Why can't computer books be easier to understand?

Not all of us want to become computer professionals, but we do want to have fun with our computers and be productive. The *Simple Guides* cover the popular topics in computing. More importantly, they are simple to understand. Each book in the series introduces the main features of a topic and shows you how to get the most from your PC.

Simple Guides – No gimmicks, no jargon, no fuss

Available in the *Simple Guides* series:

The Internet

Searching the Internet

The PC

Office 2000

Office XP

Windows 98

Windows Me

Windows XP

E-Commerce

Digital cameras, scanning and using images

Internet research

Building a website

Using e-mail

Putting audio and video on your Website

Writing for your Website

Dreamweaver 4

Dreamweaver MX

Flash 5

A simple guide to

Macromedia® Flash™ MX for Windows

Brian Salter and Naomi Langford-Wood

An imprint of PEARSON EDUCATION

Pearson Education Limited

Head Office:
Edinburgh Gate
Harlow
Essex CM20 2JE
Tel: +44 (0)1279 623623
Fax: +44 (0)1279 431059

London Office:
128 Long Acre
London WC2E 9AN
Tel: +44 (0)20 7447 2000
Fax: +44 (0)20 7447 2170
Website: www.it-minds.com

First published in Great Britain 2003
© Pearson Education Limited 2003

ISBN 0-130-45825-2

The rights of Brian Salter and Naomi Langford-Wood to be identified as the authors of this work has been asserted by them in accordance with the Copyright, Designs and Patents Act 1988.

British Library Cataloguing in Publication Data
A CIP catalogue record for this book can be obtained from the British Library.

Macromedia and Flash MX are trademarks or registered trademarks of Macromedia, Inc. in the United States and/or other countries.

10 9 8 7 6 5 4 3 2 1

Typeset by Pantek Arts Ltd, Maidstone, Kent.
Printed and bound in Great Britain by Ashford Colour Press, Gosport, Hampshire.

The Publishers' policy is to use paper manufactured from sustainable forests.

Contents

Introduction . . . .*xii*

What is in this book? xiii

Conventions and icons xiv

About the authors xiv

1 The basics 1

System requirements 2

Installation 2

Vectors vs bitmaps 6

Streaming delivery 8

Getting to know the Flash environment 8

The Timeline 11

The Stage 13

The Toolbar 14

Rulers and Grids 15

Testing your Flash MX movies 15

2 Drawing and painting 17

Creating basic shapes and objects 18
The Line tool 18
The Oval tool 20
The Rectangle tool 22
The Pencil 25
The Pen 28
Painting with the Paint Bucket 31
Painting with the Brush tool 35
The Eraser 37
The Ink Bottle 39

3 Objects 41

Selecting objects 42
    Selecting with the Arrow tool 42
    Selecting with the Lasso tool 44
    Selecting portions 46
    Deselecting parts of a selection 47
Repositioning objects 47
Simple editing commands 48
Changing line segments 50

Reshaping filled areas 51
Resizing objects 52
Reorienting objects 54
Aligning objects 56
Grouping objects 57

4 Type 59

Inserting text 60
Setting type attributes 61
Transforming type 65
Converting type to objects 65

5 Imported artwork 67

Using imported graphics in Flash 68
Acceptable file formats 68
Importing raster graphics 69
Importing vector-based graphics 71
Importing via the clipboard 71
Converting bitmaps to vector elements 73
Painting with a bitmapped image 75
Using the Magic Wand 80

6 Layers 83

Creating and deleting layers 87
Using the Layer Properties dialog box 88
    Visibility 88
    Locking 89
    Outline colours 89
    Changing a layer's height 89
    Changing the type of layer 90
Using the Timeline to control layers 92
Stacking objects on different layers 93
Guide layers 95
Mask layers 96
Paste in Place 100

7 Symbols and instances 101

Accessing libraries, symbols and instances .102
Creating symbols from graphic objects 107
Creating new symbols without conversion 108
Symbols vs objects 109
Changing an instance in an instant 110

8 Animation 115

Animation basics 116
Frame types 117
Making a simple animation 121
    Smoothing an animation 122
    Editing multiple frames 125
    Setting the frame rate 126
Motion tweening 127
    Tweening colour changes and fading in and out 131
    Tweening objects that change size 132
    Rotating objects 133
Moving objects along a predefined path 134
Shape tweening 136
Shape tweening multiple objects 140
Using shape hints to improve your morphing 141
Getting shape tweens to move along a path .143
Reversing frames 143
Animated masks 144
Saving animations 145
A note about scenes 147

9 Interactivity 149

Action types 150
Frame actions 151
Frame labels, comments and anchors 153
Some basic actions 156
Buttons 159
    Button states 160
    Creating a new button 160
Interactivity with buttons 164

10 Sound 171

How Flash handles sounds 172
Importing sounds 173
Adding sounds to frames 175
Adding sounds to buttons 176
Sync settings 177
    Adding two sounds simultaneously 179
    Start sounds 179
Streaming sounds 180
Making simple edits to your sound files 182

11 More complex interactivity and components 187

Creating a hyperlink 189
Window states 192
E-mailing from within a Flash movie 193
Components 197
Passing variables 203
Expert Mode 206

12 Publishing your movies 213

Optimising playback 214
Publishing movies for use on the Web 218
Publishing movies as stand-alone Flash player files 220
HTML publishing 224
Displaying alternative images 228
   GIF images 228
   JPEG and PNG images, and QuickTime movies 231
Projector files 232
Other image formats 232
Printing 233
   Printing from a Flash movie 235

Conclusion 239

Index 241

Introduction

Since the emergence of the World Wide Web less than a decade ago, graphic artists have demanded more and more from their software whilst also requiring fast download times for their finished masterpieces. In the past few years, Macromedia® Flash™ has become the *de facto* standard Web design tool for creating interactive animated presentations on the Internet.

Flash is now in its sixth incarnation (known as MX) and works by placing sequences of images along a Timeline, in much the same way as traditional cartoon artists produced acetate movies. Flash takes much of the effort out of the creation process by automating many of the tasks that traditional artists have had to do by hand. It also gives you total control over how the elements of the program interact with one another and with the end user.

Deceptively complex pages and animations can be put together in incredibly small files, which download very much faster than traditionally coded HTML pages. Most Web browsers support the display of Flash files, and – in short – no serious Web developer can now afford to be without it.

With the introduction of this MX version, Macromedia has made a number of changes to the way the program works. Not only have some of the keyboard shortcuts been changed since version 5, but the Panels that were introduced in that version have been changed once again. Similarly, Generator – which only came in to its own in version 5 – has disappeared altogether and been incorporated into the new Actionscript. This may well leave users of version 5 feeling frustrated that, having learned how to use that version they now have to re-learn it all over again. However, with MX the changes, though major, have made the program much more useable and straightforward.

What is in this book?

Whenever you get hold of a new program, there's always the temptation to run before you can walk. You bought Flash, after all, to get animated and interactive movies published for use on the Web or as standalone files. It can seem a bit tame, therefore, to have to learn how to construct simple graphics first; but Flash is not one of those programs that you can busk your way through – at least not if you want to make full use of the tremendous power of the software.

So, starting with the basics, this book takes you through the setting up of a Flash movie and explains all you need to know about the Flash environment. Very soon we're off using the drawing and painting tools and learning how to handle objects, insert text and import artwork from other programs.

The fun stuff then comes with the discovery of layers and the use of symbols and putting them to work in creating first basic, and then more complex animation, coupled with interactivity and sound.

Finally, it's important to know how Flash can deliver your movies to an audience – via the Web, as standalone projectors or even as alternative file formats such as animated GIFs and QuickTime or AVI movie files.

Throughout the book there are copious screen shots to help you grasp what is a complex program, quickly and easily.

Conventions and icons

Throughout the book we have included notes, each of which is associated with an icon:

These notes provide additional information about the subject concerned.

These notes warn you of the risks associated with a particular action and, where necessary, show you how to avoid any pitfalls.

These notes indicate a variety of shortcuts: keyboard shortcuts, 'Wizard' options, techniques reserved for experts, etc.

About the authors

Brian Salter and Naomi Langford-Wood are 21st century business experts and practical visionaries. Having come from very different backgrounds, they are specialists in all aspects of communication and business usage of Internet technologies and eBusiness and the building of powerful online communities; and they are leading international speakers in this arena.

Because of these core skills, they have increasingly found their company (Topspin™ Group – **www.topspin-group.com**) in demand for advice on the use of emerging technologies within business, and – in the process – recognised that the cornerstone requirement for all of this commenced with conducting client Internet and communications audits, as a prerequisite to creating effective market positioning and customer-focused Internet strategies for these clients. This approach has led to commissions by companies worldwide – both 'Blue Chip' and SMEs – to undertake Internet audits and consultations for them.

Together, Brian and Naomi help companies realise their full potential by incorporating the new technologies into their business processes as painlessly and profitably as possible whilst looking after each company's core assets – its people. Founders of The Association of E-Business Professionals, they are also fellows of the RSA and IoD.

The basics

System requirements

Installation

Vector vs bitmaps

Streaming delivery

Getting to know the Flash environment

The Timeline

The Stage

The Toolbar

Rulers and Grids

Testing your Flash MX movies

1

System requirements

Macromedia® Flash™ is a powerful authoring environment for creating animated vector graphics, and as such requires a minimum hardware configuration of:

- A Pentium 200 MHz processor running Windows 98SE, ME, 2000, NT4 or XP.
- 64 MB of RAM.
- 85 MB of available disk space.

Although Flash will work with such a configuration, the faster the processor and the larger the amount of available memory, the quicker and easier the software will be to work with.

Installation

To install Flash MX, insert the CD-ROM into your drive and the *autorun* feature should start off the InstallShield Wizard which starts extracting the set-up files automatically.

*If autorun isn't set up to work on your computer for any reason, then simply use Windows Explorer to find either the **autorun.exe** file or **Flash MX Installer.exe** on the CD-ROM and double-click on one of them, whence installation will begin.*

Figure 1.1 The opening screen of Flash MX's installation.

Once the installation files have been extracted, you are asked to close down any other programs that are running, and are then given a screen full of text that spells out the licence agreement.

To enable the software to load, you have to fill in your name and serial number (Figure 1.2). The FLW600 number that it asks for will be attached to the back of the envelope containing the installation CD-ROM, as well as on your customer registration card. You can also give the name of your organisation, if appropriate. Remember to copy the serial number exactly as it is written, complete with hyphens. When you have entered it correctly, a green tick appears to show you have entered it correctly.

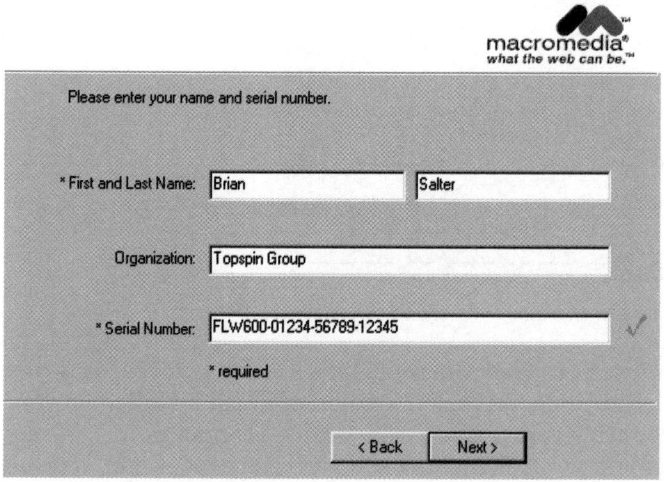

Figure 1.2 Once your details are entered correctly, a tick appears to show that you can carry on.

Next, the installation software suggests that it loads the main program into your *Program Files:Macromedia* directory, but you can choose a new destination folder if you want to by clicking on the **Browse** button and selecting a new directory path (Figure 1.3).

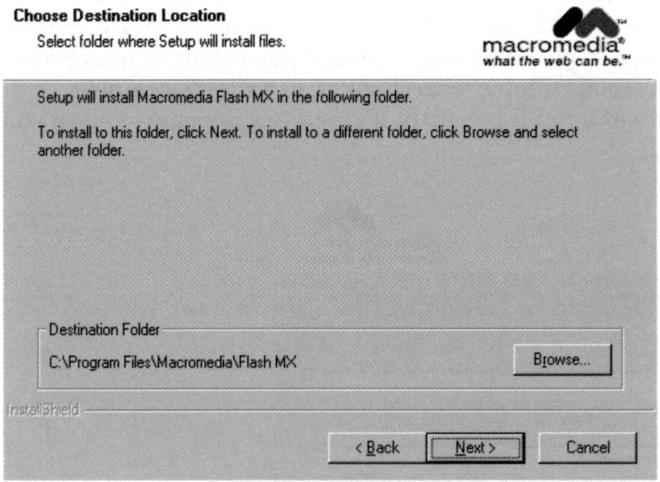

Figure 1.3 You choose where you want the software to be installed.

You are also asked if you want to load Macromedia's Flash Player for Internet Explorer. Even if you already have an earlier version of Flash installed on your PC, you should still accept this version, as Flash MX files cannot play in earlier versions of the Player unless some elements have been removed. Later you can add the plug-in Flash module for Netscape Navigator and Opera.

You have now given all the information that the program needs to copy across the relevant files, and after a final confirmation screen to check if you're really, absolutely, 100% sure of your choices (Figure 1.4), installation begins!

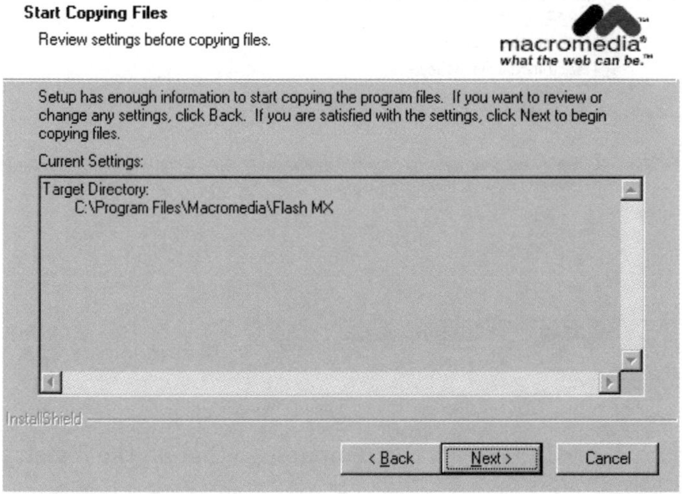

Start Copying Files

Review settings before copying files.

macromedia®
what the web can be.™

Setup has enough information to start copying the program files. If you want to review or change any settings, click Back. If you are satisfied with the settings, click Next to begin copying files.

Current Settings:

Target Directory:
    C:\Program Files\Macromedia\Flash MX

InstallShield

< Back   Next >   Cancel

Figure 1.4 Just checking (again) that you're happy with your choice of location.

Installation is pretty fast, even on the most basic hardware set-up. When the relevant files have been copied across, you should have all the shortcuts you need in your Start Menu (**Start > Programs**) (Figure 1.5), including access to the various Flash players, installers and plug-ins, not to mention, of course, the main program.

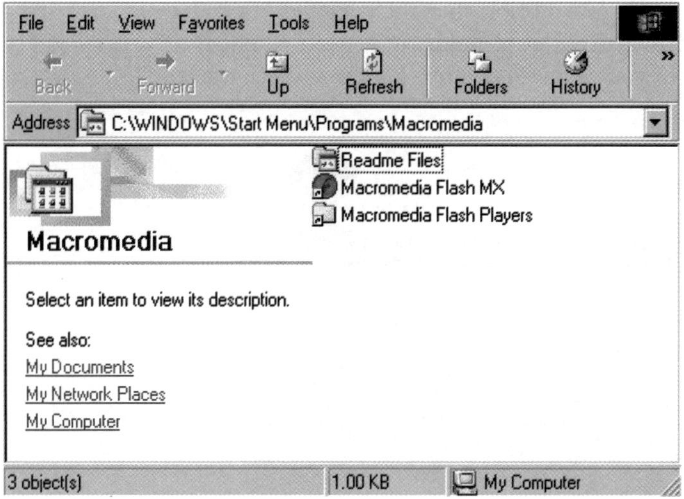

Figure 1.5 The Start Menu selection.

Before using Flash, you will need to restart the computer so that all the registry files can be set (Figure 1.6).

Vectors vs bitmaps

One of the great strengths of using Flash is that it can handle vector graphics as well as bitmapped files. It is important to understand the difference between the two for a full appreciation of the power that the software gives.

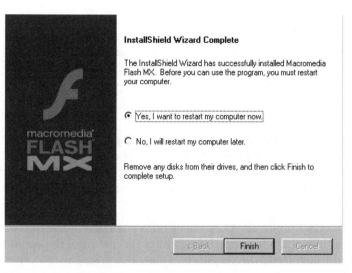

Some file formats such as .gif and .tif files can compress these instructions where there are collections of like pixels. In effect they say to the computer something such as: 'treat the next 51 pixels identically to this one'.

Figure 1.6 A quick reboot will have you up and running in no time.

Traditional image processing programs use bitmap graphics – also known as raster graphics. Here, each individual pixel of an image is defined and the computer is given instructions for each and every one of them.

The problem comes when you try to resize the graphic. Because pixels are a predetermined size that fit into a grid across your computer screen, resizing can give your image a ragged appearance.

Vector graphics, on the other hand, describe images as a series of mathematical formulae. These include lines and curves, as well as colours and position points. If you resize a vector graphic, its mathematical definition is unaltered so that the lengths of lines, or the position of certain points change, but the overall shape and quality of the graphic is unchanged.

Streaming delivery

Another of the strengths of the Flash platform is its ability to stream video or audio. With older methods of delivering such files, the user had to wait whilst the whole of the file downloaded before he could watch or listen to the file in question. Obviously, this could mean the user having to wait some time for the download, especially if it was a big file.

With Streaming, on the other hand, playback starts once a portion of the file has downloaded. Whilst you watch the first portion of video, for instance, the second portion downloads and Flash feeds the frames at a specified frame rate so that the movie appears to be uninterrupted.

Getting to know the Flash environment

When you start up Flash in order to create and edit movies, you will work with the Editor, which consists of a number of different areas with which you need to become familiar. The very first time that you start up the software, it loads one of its tutorial files, allowing you to familiarise yourself with some of the basics of the Flash MX working area. (Figure 1.7).

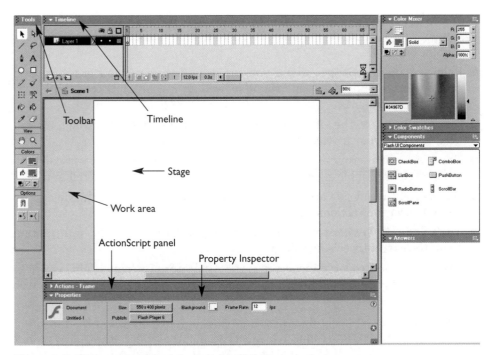

Toolbar

Timeline

Stage

Work area

ActionScript panel

Property Inspector

Figure 1.7 The main window of the Flash MX Editor.

- In the top of the window is the area known as the **Timeline**. It is here that you will store the movie's frames, layers and scenes, and organise the movie's content over time.

- Below this is the **Stage**, where you can see all your movie's graphics, and where you can import text and sound as well as navigation buttons and user-interface components.

- The **Toolbar** is to the left, where you can select the various editing tools you need to create your movie.

- The grey area surrounding the Stage is a **work area** in which you can construct various graphic elements, but which does not show in the final movie.

- On the right-hand side are **panels** that assist you in working with objects on the Stage, various actions and the Timeline.

- The **Property Inspector** at the bottom of your screen displays information about the currently selected object.

- Just above the Property Inspector is the **ActionScript** panel. This is where you use the built-in programming language to give your Flash movies rich Web content.

On all the panels and inspectors, note how there are two arrows at the top left of each (Figure 1.8). The dotted black arrow is used for dragging the panel to reposition it on your screen, whilst the white arrow opens or closes that particular panel.

*If you want to see other toolbars or Panel sets, go to the **Window** menu to determine which you want to see and which you want to hide.*

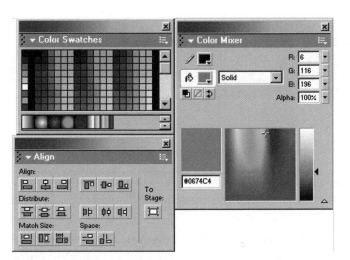

Figure 1.8 The black and white arrows are used to manipulate your panels around the screen.

The Timeline

You can think of a Flash movie in the same way as you would a film made for the 'Big Screen'. A film is made up of a series of scenes. Each scene is made up of a sequence of frames and, just as in a real film, the individual frames play sequentially to give an impression of movement.

The Timeline is where you keep the record of the components of your movie. In it, you store information about the individual frames, and assemble all the artwork into separate layers.

As with the panels, you can move the Timeline around the screen. If you dock the Timeline horizontally (i.e. at the top or bottom of the screen) you will increase the number of easily accessible frames. If you dock it to the left or right of the screen, you will see the maximum number of layers.

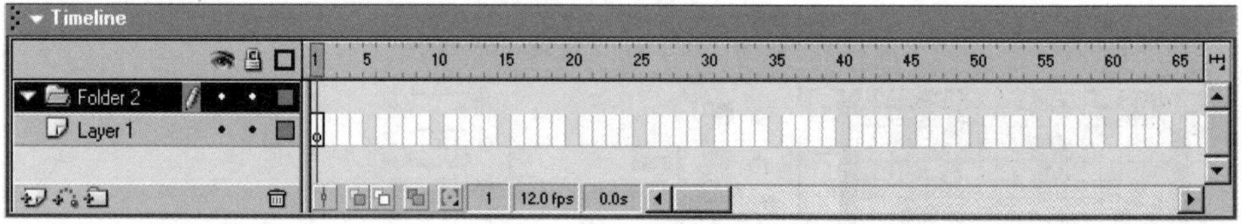

Figure 1.9 The basic Timeline.

Sometimes you will want to hide the Timeline temporarily in order to view the maximum area of Stage. In previous incarnations of Flash you would do this by choosing **Timeline** from the **View** menu or keying **Ctrl+Alt+T**. Now you can simply click on the white arrow at the top left corner of the Timeline to collapse it in on itself.

The individual layers are used to keep your artwork separate in order for you to combine them – once they are perfected individually – into a complete movie scene. With Flash MX you can now subdivide these into their own folders for ease of navigation. We'll investigate layers in Chapter 6.

Across the Timeline the frames are displayed with a 'ruler' of frame numbers along the top of the frames. In addition, the current frame number is shown at the bottom of the Timeline in the box to the left of the Frame Rate (shown as 12.0 fps in Figure 1.9).

The Stage

The Stage is the area in which you will 'Stage' your movie. It is as big or as small as you care to make it; but the size you determine will be the size seen by your audience, and will affect the relative positions of all your movie components.

You can control both the size and appearance of the Stage by double-clicking on the Frame Rate box in the status bar of the Timeline (see Figure 1.10). Alternatively choose **Modify > Document** or press **Ctrl+J**.

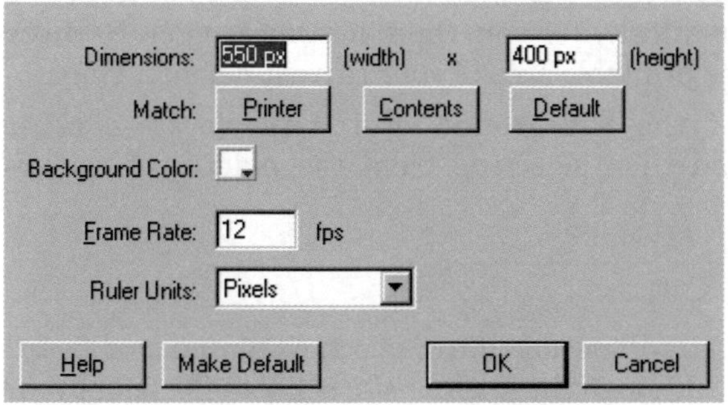

Figure 1.10 The Document Properties dialog box is accessed by double clicking the frame rate box.

You will see from Figure 1.10 that you have a number of options for the control of your Stage:

1. **Frame Rate** controls at how many frames per second the movie runs. For movies viewed over the Web, 12 is a good default. Standard films normally run at 24 fps.

2. The **Dimensions** of width and height are where you specify the overall size of the movie. You can specify the dimensions in inches, centimetres, pixels or points. Most people now view the Web in a screen resolution of 800 × 600 or 1024 × 768, although some die-hards still view it in only 640 × 480 pixels, so you will need to take this into consideration when making your decision.

3. **Ruler Units** allows you to set the units of measurement as your default. In Figure 1.10 these are set to Pixels.

4. You can set the size of the Stage to suit the contents of the movie you are currently working on. Set **Match** by clicking on the **Contents** button, and the Stage will be sized automatically for you. Similarly, clicking on **Printer** will set the Stage to match the printable area of your current default printer.

5. You can set the colour of the background of the movie by clicking on **Background Color** and then selecting from the palette of colours that appears.

The Toolbar

In the Toolbar are all the tools you will need to draw, select, paint and modify artwork and objects for animation. Although the Toolbar starts life to the left of your screen, you can also dock it on the right of the screen or have it floating wherever you wish. Notice that, depending upon which of the tools in the Toolbar you have chosen, a set of modifiers is displayed at the bottom of the Toolbar.

To help you along the way, Flash gives you the option (turned **on** by default) to show '**Tooltips**' whenever you hover your mouse over an icon (Figure 1.11). You can set your preferred default by going to the **Edit** menu and selecting **Preferences**.

Figure 1.11 Tooltips helps you select the right icon.

Rulers and Grids

Together with Rulers, you can also display a Grid, both of which are ideal aids to drawing objects with exact sizes, shapes or positions. You can turn them on by selecting **Rulers** or **Grid** from the **View** menu. This menu also allows you to snap items to the Grid. This snap feature can be set to your preferences by accessing the **Edit Grid** menu, which also allows you to specify the colour of the grid and its overall grid size (Figure 1.12).

Testing your Flash MX movies

As you work through creating your Flash animations you will need to play them back to check that your animations and interactive controls are working properly. There are three basic options:

1. Simple animations and interactive controls can be checked using the Controller toolbar, which you turn on by going to **Window > Toolbars > Controller**. This can be docked with the main toolbar at the top of the screen for convenience.

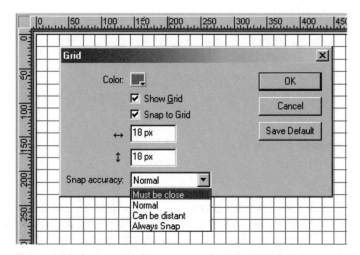

Figure 1.12 Setting your Snap accuracy from the Edit Grid menu.

2. You can access the **Test** functions from the **Control** menu.

3. You can test all your animations and controls by creating Flash Player movies that play within a separate window.

You can also publish your movie to a Web browser.

All the above are covered in detail in Chapter 12, although we will be using the checking features as we work through this book.

Drawing and painting 2

Creating basic shapes and objects

The Line tool

The Oval tool

The Rectangle tool

The Pencil

The Pen

Painting with the Paint Bucket

Painting with the Brush tool

The Eraser

The Ink Bottle

Creating basic shapes and objects

Although Flash lets you import drawings and shapes from other graphics programs, it also allows you to create your own drawings.

On the toolbar you will see a number of icons offering you access to tools such as line drawing, rectangles, ovals and so on. These allow you to create both strokes and fills for a wide variety of basic shapes. Basically, a stroke is an outline, whilst a fill is a solid. By definition, since lines have no 'insides', they consist purely of strokes. But rectangles, circles and other shapes can be either an outline (stroke) or a fill, or both.

The Line tool

Let's start with the **Line** tool. Using this, you can make simple shapes by combining a sequence of lines into, say, a star, a triangle, a pentagon, or whatever.

You can select the Line tool from the Toolbar, or by pressing **N**. Automatically, the Line Modifiers appear in the Properties panel at the bottom of the Stage, allowing you to change its colour by clicking on the coloured box (shown as a coloured square in Figure 2.1), as well as in the **Colors** panel at the bottom of the Toolbar. There is also a default black-and-white button which defaults your colour selection to two-colour mode; and beside it is another icon (shown as a two-pronged arrow in Figure 2.1) that reverses the colour selection you have made between the stroke and fill colours (we'll come to fills in a moment).

You will undoubtedly want to alter the width of the line as well as what type it is (solid, dashed, dotted, etc.) and you can set these by clicking on the **Custom** button to open the **Stroke Style** dialog box as shown in Figure 2.1.

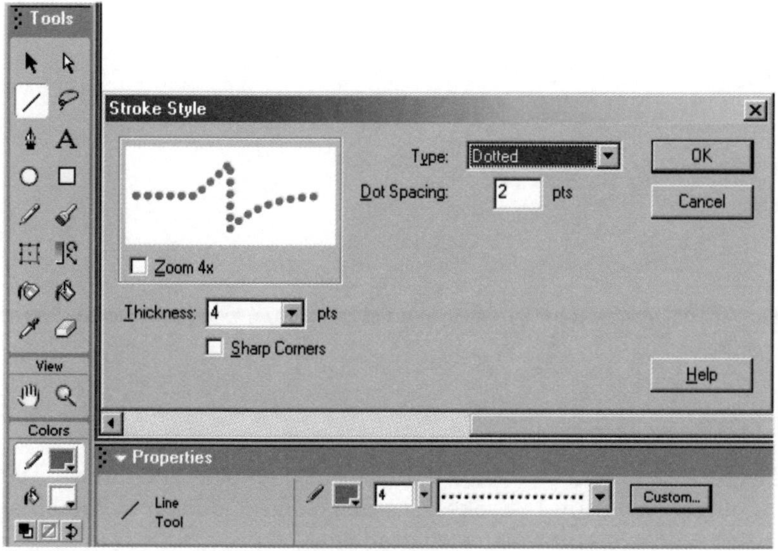

Figure 2.1 The Line tool with its Properties panel.

As you click and drag out a line, you will see a hairline representation of the line you are drawing that only turns into a line with all the attributes you assigned once you let go of the mouse button (Figure 2.2).

*If you want to constrain your line to a vertical, horizontal or 45-degree angle, hold down the **Shift** key as you drag your line.*

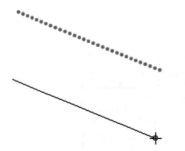

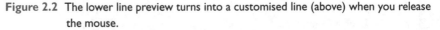

Figure 2.2 The lower line preview turns into a customised line (above) when you release the mouse.

The Oval tool

As you would expect, the **Oval** tool allows you to draw ellipses and circles. You can draw them purely as outlines (strokes), as fills (solid colour), or a combination of the two. You can even fill them with gradients.

You start the Oval drawing process by clicking on the appropriate tool in the Toolbar, or by keying **O** (Figure 2.3). If you want to draw a perfect circle, hold down the **Shift** key as you drag your outline.

This time, as well as setting the stroke colour, you can also set the colour for the fill. If you look at the Properties modifier, you will see you can also set the stroke and fill colours from here as well.

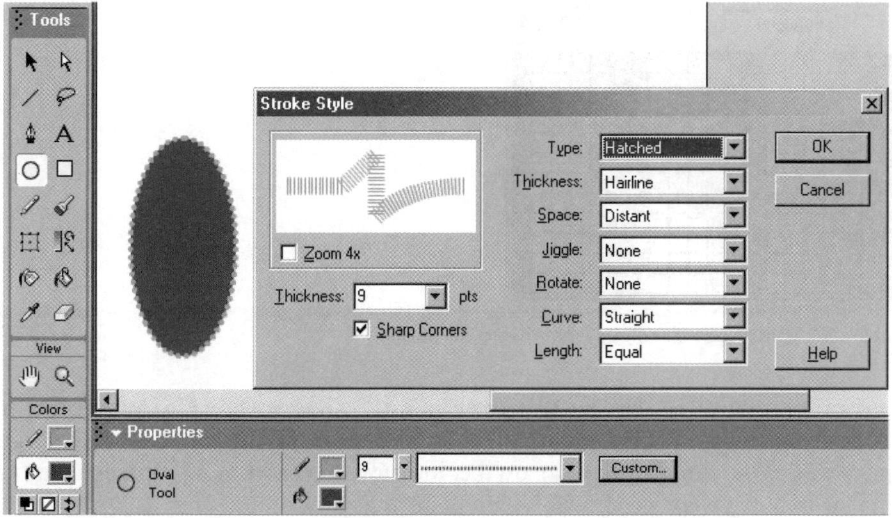

Figure 2.3 The Oval tool – with its modifier panel similar to the Line tool.

You have the option of setting either the fill or the stroke to a 'null' colour if you want to have purely a stroke or fill colour respectively. Simply click on the square icon containing a red diagonal line in the colour palette (Figure 2.4).

If, instead of a null colour, you wish to assign an actual colour, you can simply select one of the colour boxes in the colour palette. Flash encourages you to use one of the 216 'Web safe' colours – colours that can be resolved by every Web browser. However, there is nothing to stop you setting your own individual

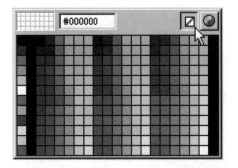

Figure 2.4 Assigning a null colour from the colour chart.

colours if you want to. In the **Window** menu, select either **Color Mixer** or **Color Swatches**, if they aren't already showing on the right of the Stage (Figure 2.5). You can define your own colour swatch, add to or replace colours in the swatch or revert to the Web-safe palette at any time.

Instead of filling an area with solid colour, you can also fill with a colour gradient. We'll cover this in more detail later in this chapter.

The Rectangle tool

*Just as with the keyboard shortcuts for Line (N) and Oval (O), you can access the Rectangle Tool simply by keying **R** on your keyboard.*

Just as with the Oval tool, the **Rectangle** tool allows you to create rectangles either as outlines, fills or a combination of the two.

This time you will see that yet another icon is introduced within the set of rectangle modifiers in the Options area at the base of the Toolbar. This icon allows

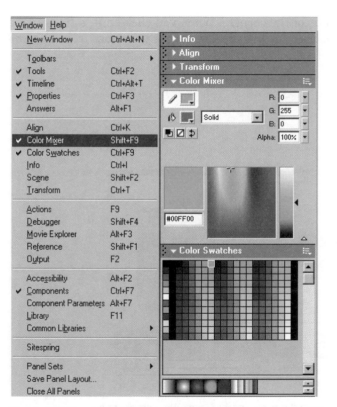

Figure 2.5 You can define your own colour scheme from the colour panels.

you to determine the radius of the corners. When you click on it, a **Rectangle Settings** dialog box appears allowing you to enter any number from 0 to 999 points (Figure 2.6).

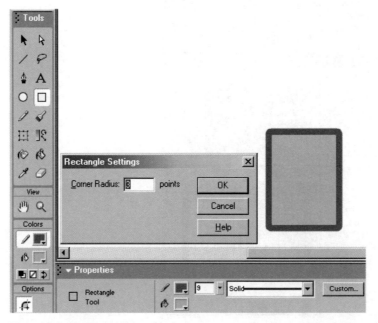

Figure 2.6 The Rectangle tool introduces yet another icon – the corner setting.

A setting of 0 will give you perfectly square corners. The higher the number entered, the rounder the corners become. In essence, what is happening is that the value you enter is the radius in points of an imaginary circle that determines the rounded corner.

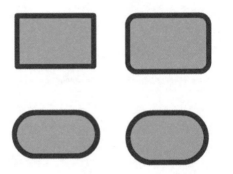

Figure 2.7 With the corner radius set to varying values, you can change the sharpness of the rectangle's corners.

The Pencil

When you use the **Pencil** tool to create lines and curves you can ask Flash to help you smooth out the wrinkles that will almost certainly occur, whether you are using a mouse cursor, a rollerball or a graphics tablet for your input (Figure 2.8).

*You can enter Pencil Mode by keying **Y** on your keyboard.*

Figure 2.8 The Pencil tool.

You do this using perhaps the most important modifier of the Pencil tool, which can be found at the bottom of the pencil toolbar. With **Straighten** mode, you can set the Pencil to straighten out the sketch you make so that, for instance, a rough rectangle turns into a perfect rectangle every time (Figure 2.9);

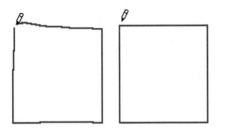

Figure 2.9 Straighten mode turns a rough sketch into a perfect rectangle.

or a wavy line can be turned into a smooth curve by selecting the **Smooth** option from the selector (Figure 2.10). Finally, you can draw freehand lines with **Ink** mode.

Figure 2.10 Smooth mode converts a wavy line into a smooth curve.

The degree of accuracy is set by selecting **Preferences** from the **Edit** menu and choosing from the selections on offer in the **Preferences** dialog box (Figure 2.11):

■ **Connect lines** allows Flash to close open circles or rectangles.

■ **Smooth curves** determines the degree of smoothing applied to a curve.

■ **Recognize lines** determines how straight a line must be before Flash converts it to a straight line segment.

■ **Recognize shapes** determines how close to a rectangle or ellipse a shape must be before Flash converts it to such an object.

■ **Click accuracy** determines how close to a line segment you must be before Flash selects it.

The Pen

In Figure 2.11 you'll also notice that there are tick boxes that allow you to determine the options for the pen tool. The **Pen** allows you to draw precise paths as straight lines or smooth or flowing curves. You can create line segments and adjust the length of the straight segments and the slope of the curved segments.

Select **Show Pen Preview** to display a preview of the line segment as you move the pointer around the Stage, before you click to create the end point of the segment.

Select **Show Solid Points** to specify that unselected anchor points appear as solid points (we'll be looking at selections in the next chapter).

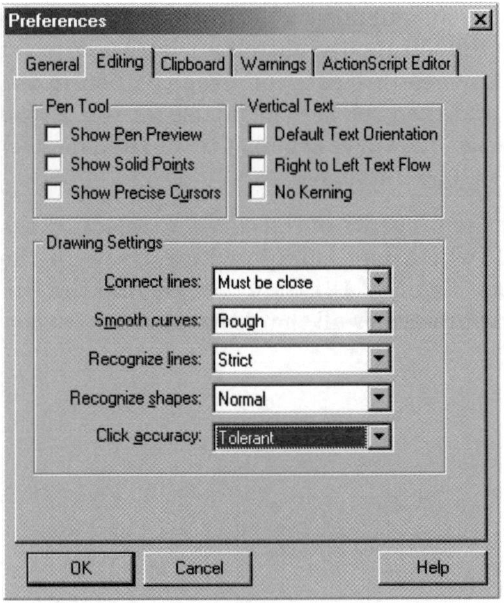

Preferences

General | **Editing** | Clipboard | Warnings | ActionScript Editor

Pen Tool
☐ Show Pen Preview
☐ Show Solid Points
☐ Show Precise Cursors

Vertical Text
☐ Default Text Orientation
☐ Right to Left Text Flow
☐ No Kerning

Drawing Settings
Connect lines: Must be close
Smooth curves: Rough
Recognize lines: Strict
Recognize shapes: Normal
Click accuracy: Tolerant

OK | Cancel | Help

Figure 2.11 Each area of the Assistant is selected using the drop-down menus.

Select **Show Precise Cursors** to specify that the Pen tool pointer appears as a cross-hair pointer, rather than the default Pen tool icon, for more precise placement of lines.

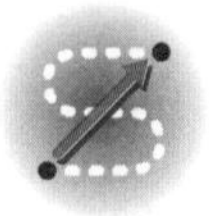

*You can press the **Caps Lock** key while working to toggle between the cross-hair pointer and the default Pen tool icon.*

To draw a curved path, select the Pen tool and position it where you want the curve to begin. Clicking and holding the left mouse button anchors your start point (the pen tip changes to an arrowhead). Next, you drag the pen in the direction you want the curve drawn and then release the mouse button. If you now position the pointer where you want the curve segment to end and double-click the mouse button, the segment will be completed.

You can move the anchor points and the tangents of the curve by selecting the curve with the **Subselection** tool (which looks like a white arrow in the Toolbar) and dragging the node points (Figure 2.12). Many people find the Pen tool hard to master at first, but a little practice is all that is necessary.

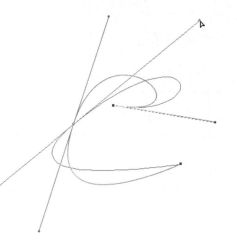

Figure 2.12 The Subselector tool is used to adjust curves.

Painting with the Paint Bucket

We've already seen how to fill an object with colour as we create it. But what if we want to fill the object later? This is where the **Paint Bucket** tool (Figure 2.13) comes into its own. Select the Paint Bucket icon (or key **K** on the keyboard) and click the mouse cursor inside the area you wish to be filled.

Figure 2.13 The Paint Bucket Tool.

Once again the colour palette is accessed by clicking on the square coloured icon in the modifiers. As well as choosing a solid colour you can set your fill as a colour gradient.

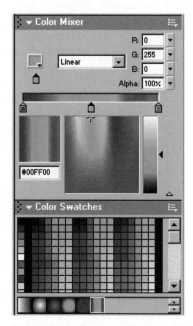

Figure 2.14 Creating a Gradient Fill.

This time you have to access the **Color Mixer** panel and choose **Linear** or **Radial** from the drop-down menu. In Figure 2.14 you can see we have selected a Linear Gradient, but you could also fill the object with your own chosen bitmap. Clicking on either end of the colour bar flags displays its present setting in the **Gradient Color** box. Clicking on this once will bring up the colour swatch for you to choose the appropriate colour; the result will be shown in the Gradient Preview window to the left. You can add extra flag points by double-clicking below the gradient preview.

Once you have created your gradient, you need to add it to your colour swatch. In the drop-down menu to the right of your Color Mixer, select **Add Swatch**. Now if you look in your **Color Swatches** dialog box, you will see a new gradient added at the bottom of your swatch. This is what you will need to use with your paint bucket.

Go back to the toolbar and select the Paint Bucket icon and then click once on the colour square in the modifiers area. A colour swatch will open up and you should see your new gradient fill at the bottom of it. Now use this tool to click anywhere inside a shape to fill it with your gradient.

Of course, you may wish to alter the angle and size of gradient that is applied to your selection. This is applied with the **Transform Fill** button (the one just above the Paint Bucket icon in Figure 2.13). As well as positioning the fill using the small white circle in the middle, you can use the top (square) handle to resize horizontally; the middle (round) handle to resize in all directions; and the lower (round) handle to rotate the direction of fill (Figure 2.15).

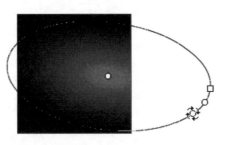

Figure 2.15 The size and angle of fill can be altered by dragging the modifier handles.

Sometimes it happens that a shape you have created is not completely enclosed. Once again, Flash comes to the rescue by making an intelligent guess as to whether you meant the shape to be enclosed or not. The **Gap Size** icon (immediately below **Options** in Figure 2.16) offers you a choice of 'closing' small, medium or large gaps.

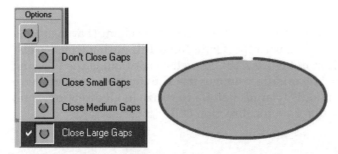

Figure 2.16 By asking Flash to close gaps for you, you can 'fill' an open shape.

Painting with the Brush tool

Flash's **Brush** tool is used for creating flows of colour – fills with no outline, if you like. You can set the shape and size of the brush by clicking on the penulti-mate two icons shown in Figure 2.17.

Figure 2.17 The Brush tool with modifiers.

Just below **Options** you will see an icon representing the Brush mode, which offers you various ways to interact with lines and shapes already on the Stage.

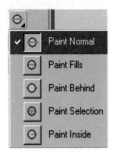

Figure 2.18 The Brush mode selector options.

Depending on the mode selected, the paint used by your Brush will affect or ignore particular areas of the Stage (Figure 2.19):

- **Paint Normal** paints over lines and fills, as long as they are on the same layer. (We'll cover layers in Chapter 6.)
- **Paint Fills** paints fills and empty areas, but does not paint over lines.
- **Paint Behind** only paints blank areas of the Stage, but leaves lines and fills unaffected.
- **Paint Selection** paints only over a selected fill. (We'll cover selections in the next chapter.)
- **Paint Inside** paints the fill area in which you start painting, but does not cross lines.

Figure 2.19 The Brush modes – Original Image, Paint Normal, Paint Fills, Paint Behind, Paint Selection, Paint Inside.

In a similar way to the Pencil tool, if you hold down the **Shift** key whilst dragging a line, it forces the Paint Brush to go either horizontally or vertically.

The Eraser

Just as you can paint using the Paint Brush, so can you erase items from the Stage using the **Eraser**. You can select whether you want your eraser round or square, and in one of five sizes.

You can erase in one of two ways:

1. By dragging using the settings offered in the **Eraser Mode** dialog box. The size and shape of the eraser is set using the drop-down menu shown at the bottom of Figure 2.20.
2. By using the **Faucet** tool (looks like a dripping tap icon).

With the former, you are offered a menu similar to the Paint Brush menu (Figure 2.21) allowing you to determine whether you want to erase fills, lines, selected fills or inside.

Figure 2.20 The Eraser tool with modifiers.

When you use the **Faucet** tool, you click on the line or filled area that you want deleted. The little drip at the end of the tap marks the point at which your selections are made, but with one click you can erase an entire line or filled shape, regardless of how many segments go into making up the strokes.

Figure 2.21 The Eraser Mode Menu Selections.

The Ink Bottle

Just as you can add a fill to an area with an outline using the paint bucket, so too can you do exactly the opposite – i.e. apply an outline – a Stroke – to an area of fill colour by using the **Ink Bottle** tool.

Having selected the colour, width and style or stroke, click the ink bottle on an area as shown in Figure 2.22.

As you can see, the fill outside the circle now has an outline to it, whilst the fill, which is inside the circle, is left alone. In other words, only the edge of the overall selection is given a new edge.

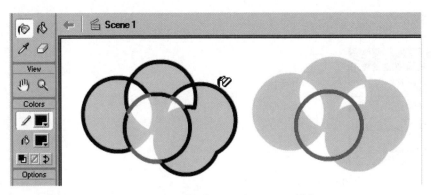

Figure 2.22 The Ink Bottle paints a Stroke round an area of Fill.

That covers the basic creation of shapes and objects. But you'll want to do a lot more than make basic shapes. Turn to Chapter 3 to see how you can make changes and improvements to what you've just done.

Objects 3

Selecting objects

Repositioning objects

Simple editing commands

Changing line segments

Reshaping filled areas

Resizing objects

Reorienting objects

Aligning objects

Grouping objects

So far, we've concentrated – naturally enough – on creating objects. But it won't be long before you will want to alter your creations in some way.

Modifying objects is an all-encompassing term. It can include:

- moving;
- colouring/re-colouring;
- straightening;
- smoothing;
- scaling;
- rotating;
- and a whole lot more besides!

Selecting objects

The first step in changing an object is to make sure it is selected, and Flash MX offers a variety of ways in which you can do this.

In common with most image-processing programs, you can use the Arrow tool to click on an object in order to select it, but you can also select items by fully enclosing them – either using a rectangular selector or a freeform lasso.

Selecting with the Arrow tool

The first thing to understand is that what you may regard as a straightforward and simple shape, is not necessarily the way that Flash MX treats it. Every time there is a twist or turn in a seemingly simple line, Flash defines a new vector path that then counts as a separate part of that line.

If, for instance, we draw a rectangle with rounded corners, Flash will treat it as four straight lines and four corners. In other words, a rectangle will be made up of eight vectors.

So let's make some selections.

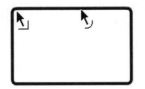

Figure 3.1 Hovering your cursor over a segment will show you what type it is.

Select the **Arrow** tool from the Toolbar and move your mouse over your intended selection (Figure 3.1). The cursor will change into either a curve point or a corner point. By simply clicking on a segment, you can select it and the segment will become highlighted. At this point, the cursor then changes once again – as you can see in Figure 3.2.

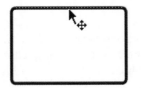

Figure 3.2 A selected segment with its associated cursor.

*If you are using another tool and you want to select the Arrow tool quickly, press the **Ctrl** key. The Arrow tool will remain your default as long as it is held down.*

To add another segment to your selection you need to hold down the **Shift** key as you select it. But if you want to select the entire shape, try double-clicking it instead. As long as all the segments are touching one another, the entire shape should become selected.

You can select a filled area in the same way you would select a line. With the Arrow tool you just click on it. The cursor changes into a selection arrow and the fill changes to a contrasting checkerboard pattern (Figure 3.3).

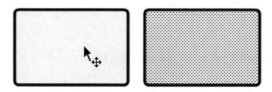

Figure 3.3 Clicking the fill (left) creates a checkerboard pattern (right).

If you want to select a group of objects – lines, corners, fills and all – the quickest method is to use the Arrow tool to drag a rectangle over the objects to be selected. Releasing the mouse selects everything inside the rectangle.

Selecting with the Lasso tool

*If you want to select everything on the Stage, you can go to the **Edit** menu and choose **Select All**. An even quicker method is to press **Ctrl+A**.*

Using the Arrow tool and drawing out rectangles is a good way of selecting objects if there is enough room between them; but if objects are close together, a safer way of selecting them is to use the **Lasso** tool, which works in a similar way to most other image-processing programs.

From the Toolbar, select the icon with the lasso on it, or simply press **L** on the keyboard. Holding the mouse key down, drag a freeform selection around the objects you wish to select and let go. Whatever is enclosed by the lasso will become selected.

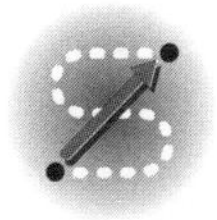

For selecting really complex shapes it can prove difficult to hold the mouse key down and drag all round the objects. Instead, Flash offers you a method that will be kinder on your hand muscles! When you select the Lasso tool, you will see a set of modifier icons appear, the lowest of which is the **Polygon mode** icon (Figure 3.4).

You don't need to close the lasso selection if you are sure that the line that would have been drawn from your end point to your start point fully encloses your intended selection.

Figure 3.4 The Polygon mode icon is shown at the bottom of the lasso selection panel.

If you select this before making your selection you will find that you can click your way around a shape adding segments as you go along. To close the selection process, double-click your mouse. You can even combine the two lasso operations by temporarily holding down the **Alt** key whilst using the Lasso, whence you will be taken to Polygon mode for as long as you hold down Alt.

Selecting portions

There are times when you will only want to select part of an element, and this is done using the **Arrow** or **Lasso** tools to enclose the areas in which you are interested.

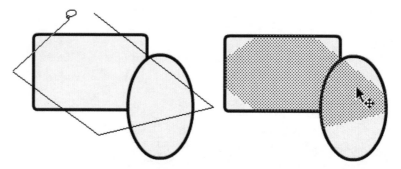

Figure 3.5 Selecting over the objects (left) creates a partial selection (right).

Deselecting parts of a selection

We've seen how you can select objects in a variety of ways in Flash. Deselecting an object is much simpler. All you need to do is use the Arrow tool and **Shift**-click the partial selection.

To deselect everything you can use one of three methods:

1. Go to the **Edit** menu and choose **Deselect All**.
2. Key **Shift+Ctrl+A** (all together).
3. Click in an empty area of the Stage.

So now that we've seen how to select and deselect items on our Stage, the next question is: what can we do with our selections?

Repositioning objects

Once you have drawn an object, the chances are that you will want to position it accurately to line up with other items on your Stage.

The quickest (and crudest) method is to click on the object with the arrow key and drag it to a new position. To help you position objects more accurately, you might care to switch on the rulers by going to the **View** menu and selecting **Rulers**. You could also switch on the positioning grid with **View > Grid > Show Grid**.

For more accuracy you could select the arrow key and click on the object, but then use the four cursor keys to move the object horizontally or vertically, one pixel at a time. (If you hold down the **Shift** key as you do this, the object will move ten pixels at a time.)

If you want to specify exactly where the item should go you can instead use the **Info panel**. If it is not already positioned on the right-hand side of your Stage go to the **Window** menu and select **Info** (Figure 3.6).

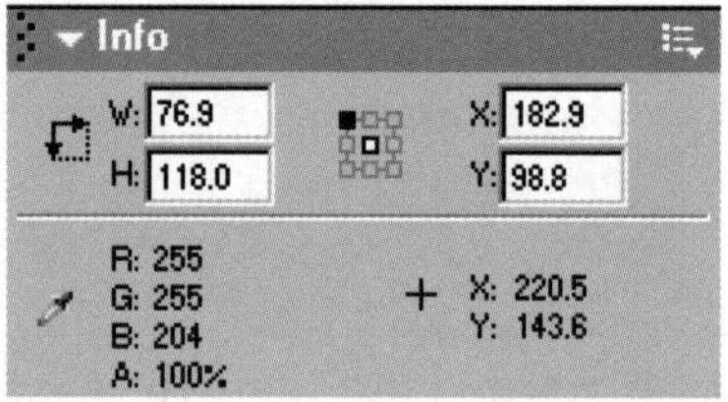

Figure 3.6 Using the Info panel to reposition an object.

Here you can see that it is a simple matter of entering x and y coordinates for accurate placement of an object. The coordinate points refer to the top left-hand corner of the object's boundary. The Info panel also contains a small grid, with a black square that indicates the registration point. If the black square is not in the upper left corner of the grid, you can click the upper left square to move the registration point there.

Simple editing commands

In common with most Windows programs, Flash supports the standard Cut, Copy and Paste options. It also has a couple of aces up its sleeve to simplify the process further.

- To **Delete** a selection – select the elements you want to delete and press either the **Delete** or **Backspace** key (or go to the **Edit** menu and choose **Clear**). Flash removes your selection.

- To **Cut** a selection – select the elements and key **Ctrl+X** (or **Edit > Cut**). The selection is copied to the Clipboard and removed from the Stage.

- To **Copy** a selection – select the elements and key **Ctrl+C** (or **Edit > Copy**). The selection is copied to the Clipboard.

- To **Paste** the Clipboard contents to the centre of your current view, press **Ctrl+V** (or **Edit > Paste**).

Sometimes it will be important to paste the clipboard contents in their original location – when you are creating multi-layered objects and exact positioning on another layer is crucial, for instance. For this version of pasting, key **Ctrl+Shift+V**, or from the **Edit** menu select **Paste in Place**.

You can **Duplicate** an object by pressing **Ctrl+D** (or using **Edit > Duplicate**). Although this doesn't change the contents of the Clipboard, it duplicates the original – offset – so that you can see both the original and the duplicate (Figure 3.7).

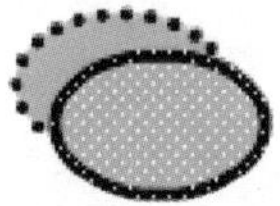

Figure 3.7 Duplicating an object offsets the copy and selects it by default.

*Instead of using **Copy** and **Paste**, you can instead hold the **Ctrl** key down whilst dragging an object. A new copy of the item appears with the original left intact.*

There is one more Paste command – **Paste Special** – that allows you to paste in objects from other programs, but which links the two. This allows you to edit the object in another program and immediately translate those changes to the object in Flash. We'll look at this in Chapter 5.

Changing line segments

Once drawn, you can use the Arrow tool to grab and reposition the end points of a straight line or curve. This allows you to lengthen or shorten them until they accurately reflect what you want.

Flash also allows you to change the direction of a line segment by dragging the end of the line to a new position, or to change the direction of the end of a curve by dragging its end in a similar manner.

But you can also change the shape of a curve, or turn a straight line into a curve by grabbing a segment in the middle of a run and dragging it to a new position. Flash automatically redraws the curve (Figure 3.8).

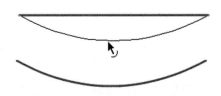

Figure 3.8 Dragging the centre of a straight line (top) until you get the outline you want (middle) creates a curve (bottom).

If you want to create a new corner point, rather than a curve, repeat the above, but hold down the **Ctrl** key as you do it. The shape of the new curve will depend on the shape you started with, but with a little practice you will soon see what a powerful feature this is (Figure 3.10).

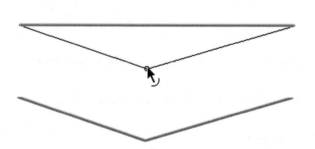

Figure 3.9 Holding down Ctrl whilst dragging produces new corner points.

Reshaping filled areas

Just as you can change the shapes of lines and curves, so too can you change the shape of a filled area. Although you can't see the edges of Fills, unless they have a stroked outline, they do nevertheless have their own (invisible) outlines.

This means that you can select their curve points or corner points and distort them just as you would a stroked outline.

Figure 3.10 Here a circular fill has its right hand edge dragged out to a new shape.

Resizing objects

Flash enables you to resize an object in one of four ways:

1. You can use the **Free Transform** tool in **Scale** mode to drag out the dimensions.
2. You can go to the **Modify > Transform > Scale and Rotate** menu.
3. You can use the **Info panel**.
4. You can use the **Transform panel**.

1. Select your object using the **Free Transform** tool, and you will be presented with a resize icon in the Options panel. Selecting this will allow you to resize your selection with resizing handles (Figure 3.11).

   By dragging out the central handles, you can resize either horizontally or vertically. Dragging one of the corner handles, on the other hand, resizes in both directions so that your aspect ratio remains the same.

2. To resize an object using the Scale and Rotate command, go to the **Modify** menu and choose **Transform > Scale and Rotate** (Figure 3.12). If you add a percentage greater than 100%, the object will be uniformly magnified. To reduce its size, however, you enter a number less than 100%.

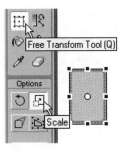

Figure 3.11 The Free Transform tool with the Scale icon selected.

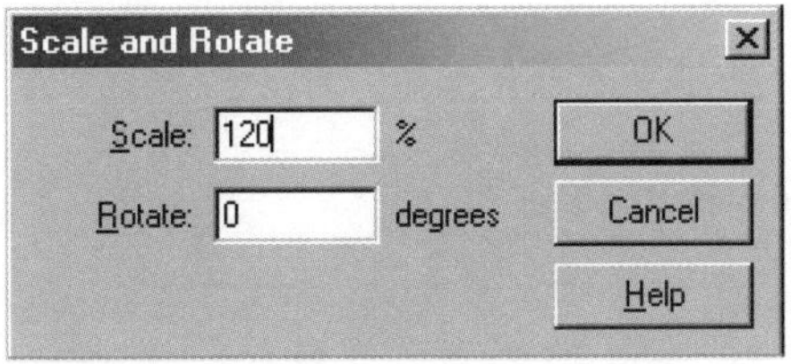

Scale and Rotate   [X]

Scale: [120] %   [OK]

Rotate: [0]   degrees [Cancel]

[Help]

Figure 3.12 Using the Scale and Rotate dialog box.

3. When we considered repositioning an object earlier on, we saw that one can use the **Info panel** to enter coordinates (see Figure 3.6). You can use this same tool to enter width and height settings – remembering that if you want to scale an object keeping its aspect ratio constant then you'll have to work out the correct ratio of W:H settings.

4. Open the **Transform panel**, if it is not already open, by going to the **Window** menu and choosing **Transform** (Figure 3.13). Having selected your object, you need to select the check box labelled **Constrain** if you want your object resized proportionally and then enter the percentage increase or decrease in the scale boxes. Press **Enter** to make the changes.

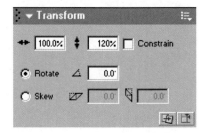

Figure 3.13 Using the Transform panel to resize an object.

If you want to resize several objects at once, make your selections first and then use any of the above four methods to convert them as one batch.

Reorienting objects

In common with most imaging programs, Flash MX allows you to **flip**, **skew**, or **rotate** an object, but once again the software comes up with a variety of ways in which you can do so. The quickest (and crudest) way is to use the **Rotate and Skew** icon on your tool bar and then to use the 'handles' attached to your selection outlines to either rotate or skew the object. In Figure 3.14, for instance, an object is selected and the Rotate and Skew icon selected, which produces an outline with 'handles' (top right). Dragging one of the corner handles rotates the object (bottom left), whilst grabbing one of the centre handles skews the object (bottom right).

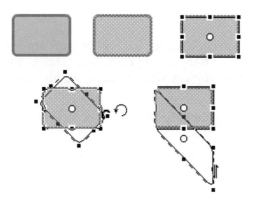

Figure 3.14 Rotating and skewing using the object's rotation handles.

If, instead of using the rotate icon, you use the scale icon next to it (Figure 3.11), you can **flip** the object – either horizontally or vertically – by grabbing one of the resulting handles and dragging it right out to the other side of the bounding box. The flipped object starts small, but grows as you continue to drag away from the bounding box.

You can rotate objects easily, either in 90-degree steps (from the **Modify** menu choose **Transform > Rotate 90° CW** [clockwise] – or **CCW** [anti-clockwise]), or by specified amounts by selecting **Modify > Transform > Scale and Rotate**; whence the dialog box we saw earlier in Figure 3.12 appears and you can just enter the degree of rotation.

Similarly you can use the **Transform** panel that we saw in Figure 3.13 to set the amount of rotation or skew.

Aligning objects

When we move on to animation techniques in Chapter 8 it will become apparent just how important it is to be able to align individual items together on the Stage. Flash allows you to align selected objects along their tops, bottoms, sides, or even by their centres.

You can even resize one object to match the dimensions of another so that they are all the same width, or height, or whatever.

You access the **Align panel** (Figure 3.15) from the **Window** menu in the normal way (if it is not already showing on the right hand side of your Stage), or by pressing **Ctrl+K** instead.

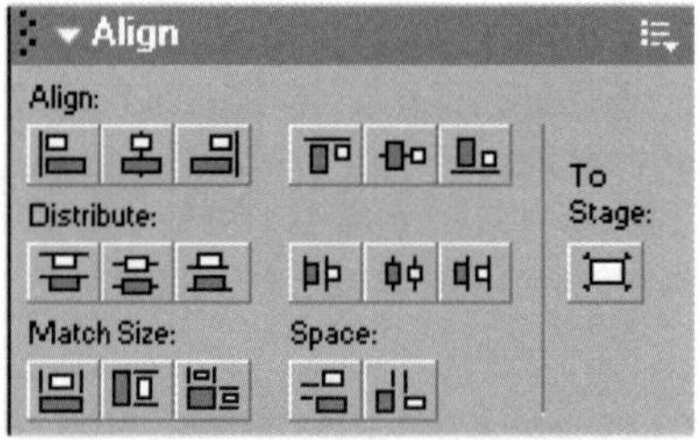

Figure 3.15 The Align panel.

Having selected the objects you want aligned, you can choose to align them vertically or horizontally via their midpoints or by either edge, as well as determining the spacing between each. The icons within the Align panel are pretty clear at showing you what is on offer. You can also **Distribute** selected objects so that their centres or edges are evenly spaced. The **Match Size** option allows you to match horizontally, vertically or proportionally with one another.

Select **To Stage** to apply alignment modifications relative to the overall Stage dimensions.

Grouping objects

As you work with a number of objects on your Stage, the time will come when you will want to regard groups of individual objects as a single object in their own right. Flash allows you to group these selected objects together by going to the **Modify** menu and selecting **Group**. A blue boundary box appears to show that the individual items are now grouped together.

Once grouped, they behave like any other single object, except that the group that you last created will be given priority in terms of appearing at the top of the 'stack' of visible objects. In other words, if you have two groups of objects that overlap, the one that was last created will appear on top of the older group.

If, having created a group, you wish to make changes to one element within the group, you can edit it by double-clicking on the grouped item, whence a flag appears in the top-left corner of the Stage informing you that you are no longer editing directly onto the Stage, but instead within the group only (Figure 3.16).

You can change the visibility order by simply selecting **Modify > Arrange > Send to Back** *(or* **Bring to Front**) *so that different grouped elements have priority.*

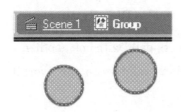

Figure 3.16 The Group 'flag' shows you are no longer editing the Scene.

When you have finished making changes to your grouped item, click once again on the **Scene** 'flag' to the left of the Group 'flag' to return to normal editing mode.

Type 4

Inserting text

Setting type attributes

Transforming type

Converting type to objects

As well as placing objects on your Stage, you will almost certainly want to use text in one form or another within your Flash environment.

The **Text** tool – represented by a capital 'A' – together with its modifiers, is what you will initially use for inserting text into your work. You can place type on a single line that expands as you type or in a fixed-width block that wraps words automatically.

Inserting text

Begin by clicking on the text tool icon and then click once anywhere on the Stage. A small box will appear with a round circle in its top right hand corner. Start typing and you'll see that as you do so, the box expands to contain the available text (Figure 4.1).

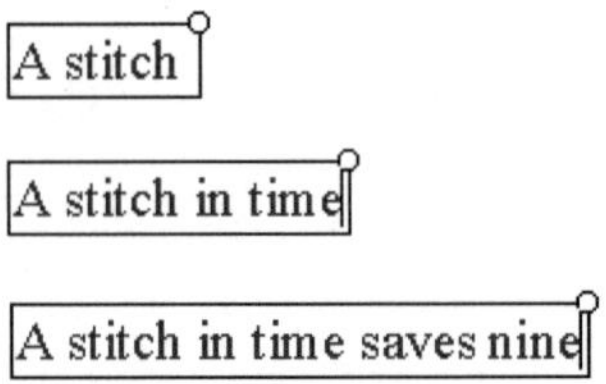

A stitch

A stitch in time

A stitch in time saves nine

Figure 4.1 The round handle in the top right corner shows there is no word wrap switched on. Note how the text box expands to accommodate the text.

To create a text block with a fixed width, however, you first need to position the pointer where you want the text to start and then drag out the box to the desired width. Instead of a circle being displayed at the top right end of the box, you should have a little square, which denotes a fixed width. Now when you type, the paragraph will automatically wrap itself around to the next line, rather than push out the limits of the box (Figure 4.2).

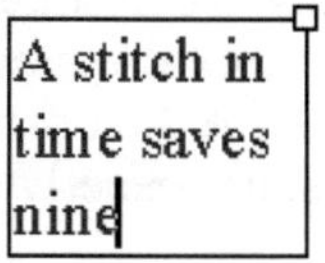

```
A stitch in
time saves
nine
```

Figure 4.2 The square handle shows that the width has been fixed.

Another way to set a finite width is to start with an expandable box – as before – but then drag the round handle to the desired width. The round handle turns square to indicate that the box width is now fixed.

Setting type attributes

Setting the weight and style of a font is comparable to that in most DTP and word-processing packages. You can set the attributes before you start typing text, or highlight text that you want to change in some way and then set its attributes.

Using the **Properties** panel (Figure 4.3), below the Stage, select the font you want, together with its size, whether you want it Bold and/or Italic, whether it should be *normal* text, *superscript* or *subscript*, and what colour the font should be.

There are other types of text field box used for interactive and dynamic text, which we shall look at in Chapter 9.

Kerning controls the spacing between pairs of characters. Many fonts have built-in kerning information. For example, the spacing between an A and a V is often less than the spacing between an A and a D.

Flash uses point size when determining the spacing between lines of text and pixels for the margin settings.

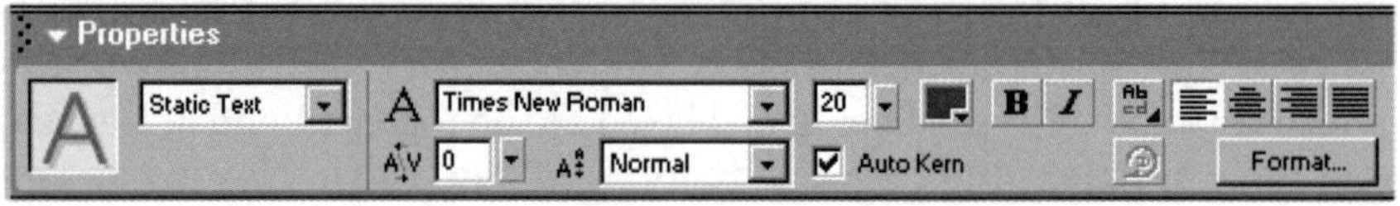

Figure 4.3 The Text Properties panel is used to set your text parameters.

When you click on the drop-down list of available fonts and hover over one of them, a representation of the text in that font will show up. You can also adjust the kerning of individual words, or of the entire text, using the **A\V** control, which might be useful for adjusting the text to fill an object or space exactly.

On the bottom right of the Text Properties dialog box is a button labelled **Format**. Clicking on this will bring up a Format Options panel which allows you to set line spacing and margins (Figure 4.4). Remember, though, that unless you show the borders of your text field in your final presentation, your audience will not be aware of the size of your margins. However, this facility may well be useful if you intend that this text should be editable in the final presentation (see Chapter 9).

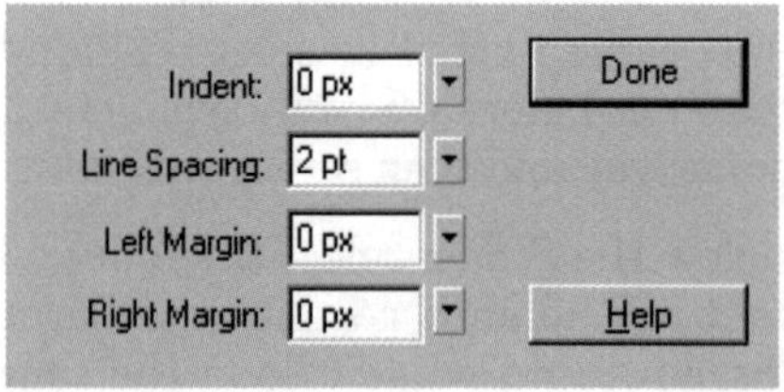

Figure 4.4 Set the line spacing and margin options from the Format Options panel.

It's very important to appreciate the difference between embedded fonts and device fonts. When you use a font installed on your system, Flash embeds the font information in the final Flash player (SWF) file, ensuring that the font displays properly in the Flash Movie.

As an alternative to embedding font information, you can use the **device fonts** that come with Flash. Device fonts are not embedded in the Flash SWF file. Instead, the Flash Player uses whatever font on the local computer most closely resembles the device font. Because device font information is not embedded, using device fonts yields a somewhat smaller Flash movie file size. In addition, device fonts can be sharper and more legible than embedded fonts at small type sizes (typically below 10 points). However, because device fonts are not embedded, if users do not have a font installed on their system that corresponds to the device font, type may appear very different from that which you have designed.

The three device fonts included with Flash are **_sans** (similar to Arial), **_serif** (similar to Times Roman), and **_typewriter** (similar to Courier). In Figure 4.5 you can see that just as with True Type fonts, hovering over a device font will give you a good representation of what that word will look like.

There are a couple of other settings you can apply from your Properties inspector. Just to the left of the Left/Centre/Right justification icons is a button that you can use to cause your text to be displayed vertically as well as horizontally (Figure 4.6). If you choose one of the vertical options, you can also then use the icon immediately below it to rotate it through 90 degrees.

*Not all fonts displayed in Flash can be exported with a movie. To verify that a font can be exported, use the **View** menu to switch between **Fast** and **Antialias text**. In the former mode, your text should look ragged, whilst if the font can be exported into a Flash movie, choosing antialias should smooth the font on screen. Jagged type indicates that Flash does not recognise that font's outline and will not export the text..*

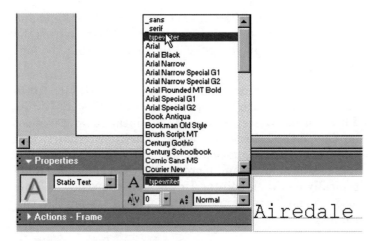

Figure 4.5 Hover over a font to see what the text will look like in your Flash movie.

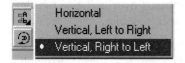
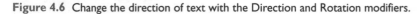

Figure 4.6 Change the direction of text with the Direction and Rotation modifiers.

Transforming type

You can transform text blocks in the same way as other objects; that is, you can scale, rotate, skew and flip text blocks to create some interesting effects. The text in a transformed text block can still be edited, although be wary of going mad with your designs as severe transformations can make the text difficult to read.

Figure 4.7 Has Brian finally flipped? Rotation and skew work on text just like any object.

Once you have converted type to line strokes and fills, you will no longer be able to edit your text.

Converting type to objects

There will be occasions when, having written text into your movie, you will want to work with it just as if it was any other object, so that – for instance – you can stretch it, distort it and paint it.

To convert your text to such an object, select it and then go to your **Modify** menu. Choose **Break Apart** and the word will be split into separate letters (Figure 4.8). Select which individual letters you now wish to manipulate and once again choose **Break Apart**. This has the effect of converting

Break Apart *applies only to outline fonts such as TrueType fonts. Bitmap fonts disappear from the screen when you break them apart.*

your text into objects. But beware! Having converted your font to an object, you can manipulate it any way you like. But it's too late now to go back and edit your text!

Figure 4.8 Once Naomi has been broken apart, she can be treated just like an object!

We'll be examining the use of objects in much more detail in Chapter 7.

Imported artwork 5

Using imported graphics in Flash

Acceptable file formats

Importing raster graphics

Importing vector-based graphics

Importing via the clipboard

Converting bitmaps to vector elements

Painting with a bitmapped image

Using the Magic Wand

Be aware that, although you can import most vector graphics, you may well find that not all the features of the vector-producing programs you use translate readily into Flash.

Using imported graphics in Flash

As well as enabling you to produce quite complex graphics, Flash MX also allows you to import graphics from other programs.

When importing graphic elements, you can import both vector graphics and raster – or bitmapped – images. So if you already use image-processing applications such as *Fireworks, Photoshop, Illustrator, Paint Shop Pro* or *CorelDraw*, you can rest assured that it is likely you will be able to utilise any existing artwork.

Flash can also import movie files, and we'll return to this later.

Acceptable file formats

There are very many file formats that Flash can handle, and the following are easily imported regardless of whether Quick Time 4 is installed on your PC:

- .emf (enhanced metafile);
- .wmf (Windows metafile);
- .dxf (AutoCAD);
- .bmp (Windows bitmap);
- .gif (Compuserve graphic image format);
- .jpg (JPEG);
- .png (Portable Network Graphics);
- .spl (FutureSplash);
- .eps & .ai (Adobe Illustrator);
- .fh? (Freehand);
- .swf (Flash player).

Flash MX can also import some extra file formats if you have QuickTime 4 or later installed on your system. This could be especially useful if you work on both Windows and Macintosh platforms. With QuickTime 4 you can import:

- .psd (Adobe Photoshop);
- .pntg (MacPaint);
- .pic/.pct (PICT);
- .tif (TIFF);
- .tga (Targa);
- .sgi (Silicon Graphics);
- .mov (QuickTime Movie);
- .qtif (Quick Time Image).

Importing raster graphics

Raster (bitmapped) graphics can easily be brought into the Flash environment by going to your **File** menu and selecting **Import**, whence an Import dialog box (as in Figure 5.1) appears.

You navigate in the normal way to the particular file on your computer system and either click **Open**, or double-click on the file in question.

Flash responds by both storing a copy of the bitmap in question on the Stage in whatever layer is currently active (see Chapter 6) as well as placing a copy of it in its library (see Chapter 7).

Sometimes you will want to import a number of sequential files for use as keyframes in a movie. (We'll cover keyframes in Chapter 8). If all the file names are identical (such as in Figure 5.1), apart from a series of sequential numbers, then Flash will ask you if you want to import all, rather than just one, image (Figure 5.2).

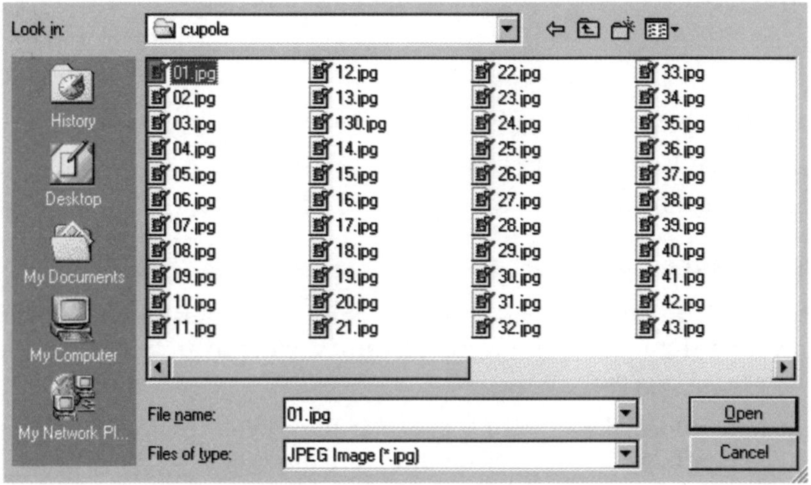

Figure 5.1 The Import dialog box.

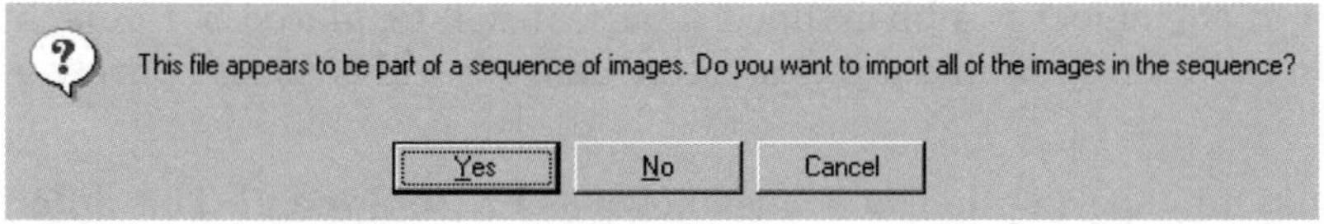

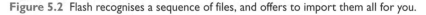

Figure 5.2 Flash recognises a sequence of files, and offers to import them all for you.

Importing vector-based graphics

Importing vector graphics is a very similar process to that used for raster graphics. The main difference lies in what Flash does with the file.

Whereas a bitmapped image is placed both on the Stage as well as in the Library, a vector image is placed on the Stage as a grouped object but it is not placed in the Library. You can **ungroup** the vector image by choosing **Modify > Ungroup**, and this allows you to work with the ungrouped object much as you would with any vector image created within Flash itself.

Importing via the clipboard

Both bitmaps and vector images can be pasted into Flash via Windows' clipboard. It's a little bit hit-and-miss, however, as vector objects in particular can lose some of their information, leading to oddities in the translation. But as a 'quick and dirty' method it is very simple.

Start by opening up the application used to create the graphic and select and copy the object (very often, though not always, using **Ctrl+C**). Open up Flash (if it is not already open) or click anywhere within the Flash environment to 'bring it alive' and click **Ctrl+V** or choose **Edit > Paste**.

When importing vector files from Adobe Illustrator and from Macromedia Fireworks, the original layers are recreated within Flash.

Once again, if the object is a bitmapped image, it will be placed both on the Stage and in the Library, whilst if it is a vector image it will be placed purely on the Stage.

Flash also has an import option, which is known as **Paste Special**. This differs from the previous use of the clipboard in that, instead of pasting the contents directly onto the Stage, Flash pastes them, at the same time as creating links to the original files. If you want to modify these items, Flash will then open up the original program where you can make your changes; anything that you then change will be reflected back in the image on Flash's Stage (Figure 5.3).

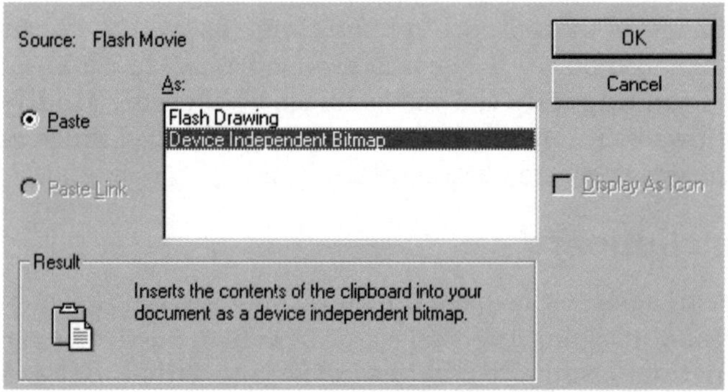

Figure 5.3 The Paste Special dialog box, which changes depending on what is in the clipboard.

Converting bitmaps to vector elements

You can convert a bitmapped image into a vector file allowing you to work on the image in exactly the same way you would any other vector object. Because photographic-type images could well end up with a massive amount of colour shadings and vector curves, it is necessary to strike a happy balance between accuracy and file manageability.

With the bitmapped image on your Stage, select **Modify > Trace Bitmap** from the file menu and a dialog box similar to that shown in Figure 5.4 will appear.

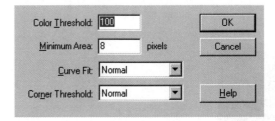

Figure 5.4 The Trace Bitmap dialog box.

As you can see, there are a number of parameters you can enter and they control how close a match your final vector image will be to the original bitmapped image.

Although Macromedia recommends that settings for photographs should be 'Color Threshold, 10; Minimum Area, 1; Curve Fit, pixels; Corner Threshold, Many corners', you are likely to end up with huge files if you follow this advice. Ask yourself why you would want to have this level of resolution in your vector object and see if you cannot find a way around it – perhaps by combining a vector and a bitmapped graphic so that only the area that needs to be vectorised is converted.

- **Color Threshold** determines the amount of similar colours that get clumped together within one vector object. With a low threshold, more individual colours are recognised, but the downside to this is that you end up with many more vector objects and a correspondingly larger file size.

- **Minimum Area** guides Flash into working with neighbouring pixels to work out a colour match. The more pixels it works with, the lower the detail and the lower the file size.

- **Curve Fit** determines the smoothness of the curved outlines around individual vector shapes.

- **Corner Threshold** guides Flash as to whether it should create sharp corners or more rounded ones.

Figure 5.5 A picture traced with a *color threshold* of 10 and a *minimum area* of 1.

Figure 5.6 The same picture traced with a *color threshold* of 50 and a *minimum area* of 20.

Painting with a bitmapped image

Bitmapped images can be used to fill other areas as a repeating pattern. You might find this useful if, for instance, you wanted to fill some text with an image pattern, or wanted to 'paint' the pattern onto the side of an object.

First select the bitmapped image on your Stage. Let's use a typical street scene in downtown Jeddah to superimpose on some objects (Figure 5.7).

Figure 5.7 First we select the bitmap.

From the **Modify** menu select **Break Apart**. You will see that the entire bitmapped image looks as if a tiny grid, similar to that shown in Figure 5.8, covers it.

If you now select the Dropper tool and click anywhere on the 'broken apart' image it will select it as a fill pattern so that it can be used in a similar way to a gradient fill. You will see that the Paint Bucket tool has been automatically selected, and that the **Fill Color** icon in the Color Mixer palette is filled with a tiny representation of the image

Figure 5.8 The bitmap is 'broken apart' waiting for the Dropper tool.

You could use this image to fill a selected area of an object. Alternatively you could try using the Paint Brush or create filled rectangles and ellipses to see the power of the software in action (see Figure 5.9). Remember, though, that you have to select Bitmap fill in the Color Mixer palette rather than a solid colour or a gradient fill.

Once you have filled your object, you might decide that you want the focus of the fill altered. Perhaps you want another part of the fill as the focus, or you want it resized.

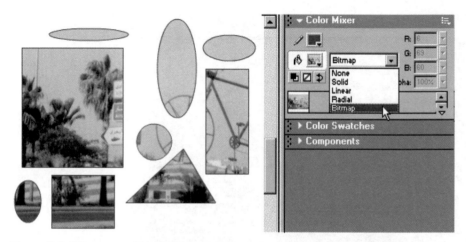

Figure 5.9 Filling areas with our original image.

To move the centre of a bitmapped fill, select the Paint Bucket tool and then choose the **transform fill** modifier positioned immediately below the Paint Brush tool in the toolbar. If you position the resulting cursor over your fill object and click, you will see handles for manipulating the object appear (Figure 5.10). You can use:

- the central handle to reposition the centre of the fill;
- the bottom centre handle to alter the height of the fill;
- the left side centre handle to alter its width;

- the bottom left corner handle to alter the size proportionally;
- the top right corner handle to rotate the object;
- the top and right centre handles to skew the object.

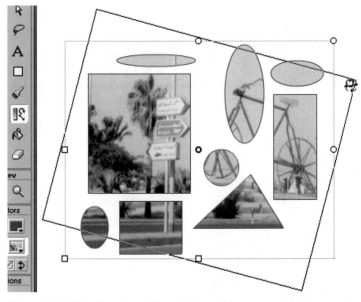

Figure 5.10 The Transform Fill modifier used to resize, shift, skew and rotate the fill.

Using the Magic Wand

You can use the **Magic Wand** tool to select areas of a bitmapped image that have like-colours. For instance, on the picture that we have been using we might want to select a patch of sky.

First you need to select the bitmapped image as before and break it into its component colours (**Modify > Break Apart**). Deselect the image.

Now choose the **Lasso** tool and select the **Magic Wand Modifier**. By clicking on particular colours of the image with your magic wand you can select whole areas of like colour. You can alter the Magic Wand's settings by clicking on the right-hand modifier. Here you can set the threshold and the smoothing levels as before (Figure 5.11).

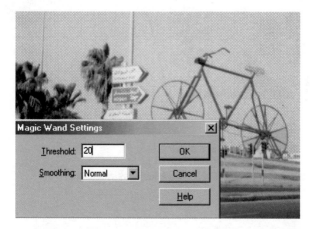

Figure 5.11 Select like areas of colour and set your threshold limits with the Magic Wand.

If you want to, you can then modify that particular area – such as painting it with solid colour or a gradient using the Bucket Fill, or even deleting portions of it so that a lower level of design comes through the 'holes' in the picture (Figure 5.12).

Figure 5.12 Having selected your areas you can use the Paint Bucket to add some special effects.

Layers 6

Creating and deleting layers

Using the Layer Properties dialog box

Using the Timeline to control layers

Stacking objects on different layers

Guide layers

Mask layers

Paste in Place

Importing and creating artwork in Flash is all very well; but you could very quickly get to the point where the workings on one section of your artwork could interfere with other aspects of your image creation. In addition, the more images that are stacked one on top of the other, the more complicated the manipulating of those images becomes.

Flash – in common with many other image creation programs – uses **Layers** to circumvent this problem. Think of a pad made up of a number of sheets of tracing paper; but instead of being translucent, you can see clearly through each one. Each different sheet has a separate part of the image you are working on and you can arrange for separate sheets to hide or display the work underneath their own. You can move the layers around in any order and you can move the objects within each layer.

The main power of layers lies in the fact that you can edit or manipulate the objects on a particular layer without affecting any of the objects on other layers; or, in addition, you can get the objects on one particular layer to affect the objects on another layer in some predetermined way.

With the release of Flash MX, Macromedia has also provided **Folders** in which to store your layers. This way, if you have many layers, you now don't have to scroll up and down looking frantically for that one layer hidden in a mass of others. Instead, you could have graphics in one folder, images in another, sounds in a third, actions in a fourth, and so on.

And when it comes to animating your movie, layers really come into their own by providing the facility to move objects along pre-defined paths. We'll deal with animations in Chapter 8.

Flash gives a visual representation of each layer at the start of the Timeline. When you start up Flash there will, of course, be only one layer since you have yet to create any. You can see in Figure 6.1 that there is a selection of icons associated with the layer Timeline. We'll come to the use of the top three icons in a short while. For the moment, though, you will notice three icons in the bottom left hand corner which are used for creating *new layers*, *new guide layers* and *new folders*, respectively. On the bottom right-hand side is a dustbin (or trashcan) icon used for *deleting* layers or folders.

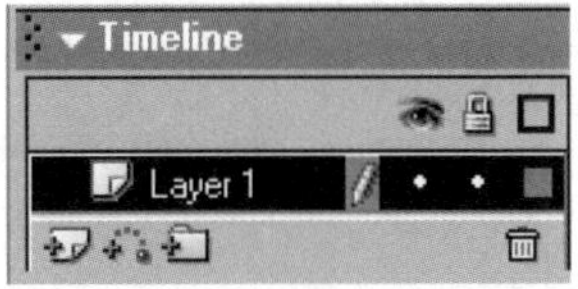

Figure 6.1 Flash begins with one layer.

You will also see that, by default, Flash has called your base layer '*Layer 1*'. As each new layer is created, it will be given a number equivalent to the amount of new layers created (not necessarily the number of layers in existence, since you might have deleted or merged some).

You can easily rename these layers and, in fact, it is probably best to do so since as you create more and more layers it is easy to lose track of where you are.

To rename a layer, simply double-click on the name and type in a new one.

There is another way to rename your layer, and that is via the **Layer Properties** dialog box. We'll be returning to this dialog box throughout this chapter. To access it, go to the **Modify** menu and click on **Layer**, or right-click on the layer itself and choose **Properties**, or double-click on either the **sheet** icon (next to 'Layer 1' in Figure 6.1) or the **solid square** icon at the right-hand end of the 'Layer 1' layer. The dialog box that opens will be similar to that shown in Figure 6.2.

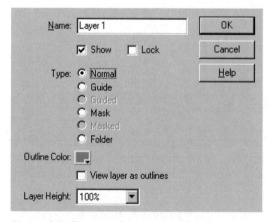

Figure 6.2 The Layer Properties dialog box.

The first field is where you can type in a name for the layer. In fact, when the box appears, you will see the name is already highlighted, waiting for you to type in your new name straight away.

Creating and deleting layers

It is normal to create layers on-the-fly as you need them, although there is no reason why you could not create a number of layers to start off with and then work on them individually after that.

You can create layers in a number of ways. The simplest is to click on the left-hand icon at the bottom left of the Timeline that we saw in Figure 6.1. However, you could also choose **Layer** from the **Insert** menu (Figure 6.3) or press **Alt+I**, **Alt+L**.

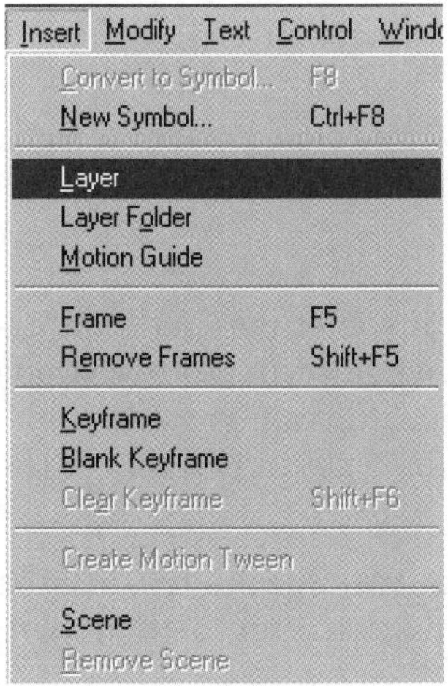

Figure 6.3 Inserting a new layer via the menu bar.

*If you want to delete more than one layer at a time, make a selection of layers together holding down the **Ctrl** key as you do so, and then click on the dustbin.*

Flash will always create a new layer above the currently selected layer, so it is important to think where in the stacking order you want your new layer to appear.

Which is the current layer? If you look at Figure 6.1 you will see that Layer 1 has a black background, as well as having a pencil icon. (We'll return to that pencil in a moment.) All the layers that are not the currently selected one will have a grey background.

Deleting a layer is just as easy. Select the layer by clicking on it and then either drag it to the dustbin or just click on the dustbin.

Alternatively, right-click on the layer itself and select **Delete Layer**.

Using the Layer Properties dialog box

We saw in Figure 6.2 that you can use the Layer Properties dialog box to rename a particular layer. It can also be used to set other parameters for that layer.

Visibility

For instance, when you have objects on many layers, it sometimes gets confusing to have all the layers visible on the Stage at once when trying to tweak one small aspect of a particular object. To aid you in your editing, you can make any of the layers temporarily invisible so that they don't get in the way of the object you are trying to see.

You will see in Figure 6.2 that the second row has two checkboxes. If the **Show** box has a tick, then the layer will be visible; no tick, and the layer will become invisible.

Locking

Similarly, once you have worked on an object you may wish to protect it from accidental changes made when editing another object. In this instance, if you tick the **Lock** box, it will protect that layer from any further changes. When the layer is locked, you can still see the objects, but you cannot select them or edit them.

Outline Colours

You will see one of the options allows you to view the contents of a layer as a set of outlines and to change the outline colour. In order to aid the placing of objects on the Stage relative to one another, Flash gives you the option of displaying purely the outlines of objects. To do so, tick the checkbox marked **View layer as outlines**.

So that you can determine which outlines are on which layers, you can colour-code the outlines so that, for instance, the outlines of objects on Layer 1 could be in red, Layer 2 in green, and so on.

Clicking on the coloured rectangle above **Outline Color** will bring up a colour palette from which you can choose whichever colour you wish (see Figure 6.4).

Changing a layer's height

The lowest box in the Layer Properties dialog box allows you to alter the height of the layer bars in the Timeline. This is especially useful if you want to view the waveforms of sound channels, which are hard to see at the normal 100% setting (see Chapter 10).

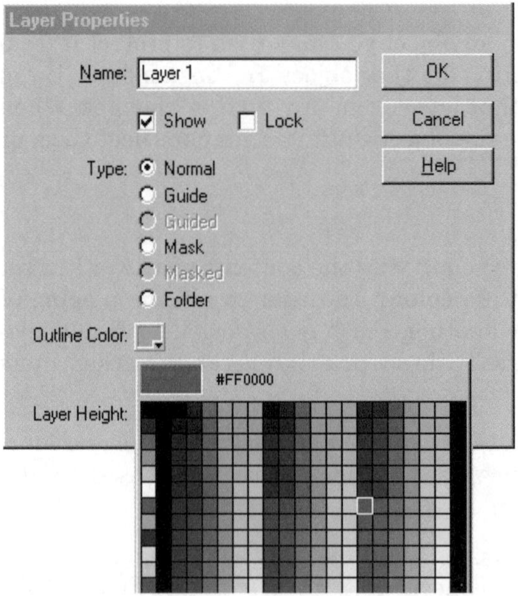

Figure 6.4 Changing the outline colours of your wire frames.

Changing the type of layer

You will have noticed that the middle of the Layer Properties dialog box is taken up with a series of radio buttons allowing you to determine the type of layer you wish to work on.

You can set a layer as:

1. Normal;
2. Guide;
3. Guided;
4. Mask;
5. Masked;
6. Folder.

In addition, a layer can be a Motion Guide layer, which we will look at in Chapter 8.

1. The **Normal** layer is the default, and all objects in a normal layer will appear in your final movie.
2. **Guide** layer objects do not appear in a final movie. They are there purely to guide objects on other layers to be positioned accurately, or to move in a particular direction or path.
3. A **Guided** layer is aligned to a guide layer and reacts according to its settings.
4. A **Mask** layer can either hide or reveal the contents of layers lying below in the stacking order.
5. These lower layers are called **Masked** layers.
6. A **Folder** contains layers stacked beneath it. You assign layers to their respective folders by dragging the particular layer and 'dropping' it on the selected folder.

In the Timeline, these different layers are shown with different label icons, as shown in Figure 6.5.

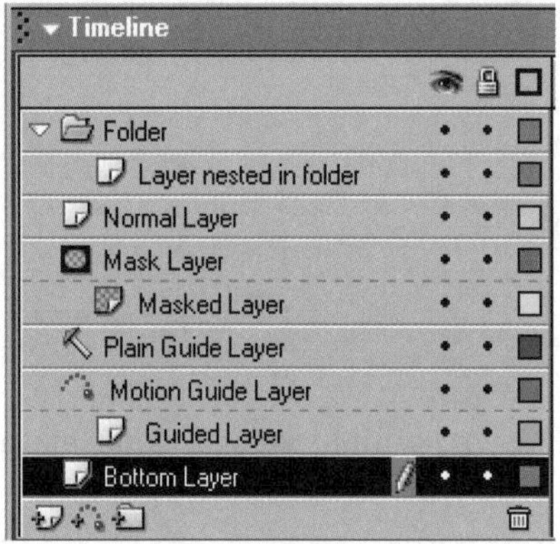

Figure 6.5 Each type of layer has its own individual icon.

Using the Timeline to control layers

Many of the controls we talked about in the previous section can be more easily achieved by clicking on icons in the Timeline.

If you look at Figure 6.6, you will see three icons in the top right-hand corner, which are, respectively,

1. visibility;
2. locking;
3. outlines.

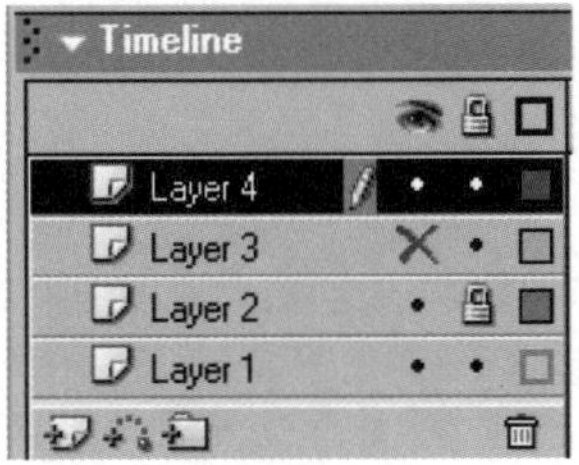

Figure 6.6 Control icons in the Timeline.

If you click on a bullet below the 'eye' icon, the bullet will turn into a red cross sign, and that layer will no longer be visible.

Click on a bullet below the padlock icon, and the bullet turns into a padlock. Now, any objects on that particular layer are protected from being edited.

A click on a filled square below the square icon itself turns into an empty square, leaving all objects in that layer shown as outlines only. The colour of the square is representative of the colour of the layer's outlines.

Stacking objects on different layers

When you place objects on different layers, those in the higher layer levels will always appear 'on top' of the lower objects.

Suppose you have three shapes – a lozenge, a square and a circle placed on Layers 3, 2 and 1, respectively. As you will see in Figure 6.7, the square is placed over the circle, whilst both are eclipsed by the lozenge.

If you want to change the visibility, lock or outline properties of a number of consecutive layers in one go, click a bullet on the first layer and drag the mouse button through all the other layers.

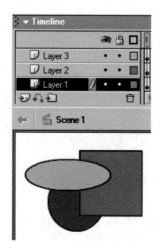

Figure 6.7 Three objects are stacked in the order of their respective layers.

If we now grab the individual layers and drag them into a new order, as shown in Figure 6.8, you will see that the stacking order of the objects changes accordingly.

Although only one layer may be selected at any time, this does not mean you cannot edit items on other layers. For instance, if you were to have a Stage set up as shown in Figure 6.8, you could select the paint bucket tool and click on each of the shapes in turn – without having to select and deselect layers – in order to fill each shape with a new colour.

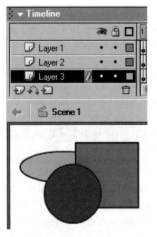

Figure 6.8 Reverse the layer order, and the stacking changes too.

Guide layers

We've already identified that there are two types of Guide layers:

1. Plain Guide layers;
2. Motion Guide layers.

We will return to Motion Guides in Chapter 8; to create a Plain Guide layer, however, you have to convert an existing layer into a Plain Guide layer. (You will remember that we can convert a layer in this way by going to the Layer Properties dialog box and clicking on the appropriate radio button.)

*You can also create a Guide layer by right-clicking the layer you want to define as a guide and choosing **Guide** from the pop-up menu.*

It's a good idea to lock Guide layers once you have set them up, so that you don't accidentally move the guides as you work with other layers.

There are many things you might wish to do with Guide layers. For instance, you could place any objects on a guide layer to act as reference points when placing objects on other layers. These objects are not included in the final movie, however; they merely act as guides.

One particularly good use for Guide layers is to place guidelines on them, similar to the guidelines used by page-layout programs such as Quark Xpress. By using the **Snap to objects** feature (turned on by default in your **View** menu) you can then line up individual items to the guidelines in your Guide layer.

Mask layers

A **Mask layer** allows you to hide elements selectively in other layers that are linked to it – that is elements in *Masked layers*. You can think of a Mask layer as an opaque sheet that has holes cut in it to allow you to see exactly what is underneath those holes, but no more.

Although it is possible to create an animated mask so that the window 'moves' over the Masked layer, we'll stick for the moment with a static mask. (We'll cover animated masks in Chapter 8.)

There is no such thing as a semi-transparent hole; so too can a mask either be applied or not. There is no such thing as a semi-transparent mask. What this means in practice is that anything you put down on your Mask layer will allow whatever is on the Masked layer to show through. Any areas of the Mask layer left untouched will block out what is contained underneath on the Masked layer.

To show this in practice, consider Figure 6.9. Here we have created two plain layers. A rectangle is drawn on Layer 1 and an oval on Layer 2. We have filled the oval with a gradient running from black to green.

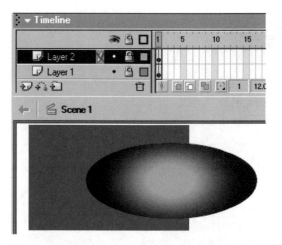

Figure 6.9 Two plain layers containing a rectangle and oval respectively.

If we now convert Layer 2 into a Mask layer (right-click on the name 'Layer 2' and select **Mask**) and Layer 1 into its Masked layer (in this case, as there are only two layers, Layer 1 automatically becomes the Masked layer) you will see in Figure 6.10 that the area of the rectangle overlapped by the oval is visible, whilst the remainder of the rectangle is hidden.

Notice, too, that the amount of shading within the oval makes no difference to the amount of rectangle that is visible.

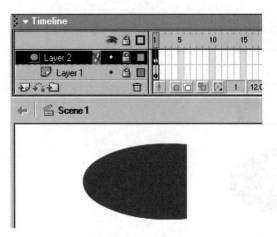

Figure 6.10 Layer 2 is now a Mask layer, with Layer 1 the corresponding Masked layer.

If you want to make more than one Masked layer attributable to one Mask layer, you have to go to the Layer Properties dialog box and then click on the radio button marked **Masked**, having first positioned the layer immediately below the Mask layer.

In Figure 6.11 you can see that the Mask layer is shown with a 'griddled egg on a black background' as its icon, whilst the Masked layers each have a griddled page icon and are indented below the Mask layer.

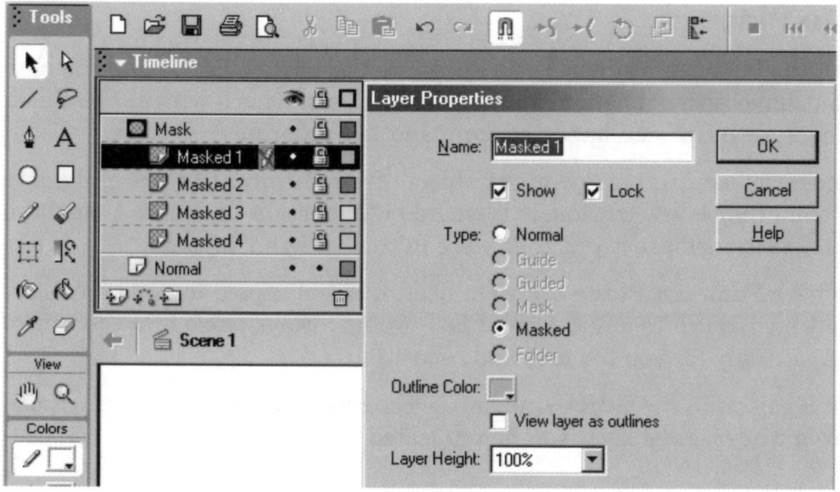

Figure 6.11 Each of the Masked layers is indented.

When you create a Mask layer with its Masked sub-layer(s) you may not see anything different at first. This is because, for the masking to work, you have to lock the Mask layer and *all* Masked layers beneath before masking takes effect. (Look for the little padlock icon on each layer showing its lock status.)

A quick and easy way to create extra Masked layers is to drag existing layers directly underneath the Mask layer, or to select one of the Masked layers and create a New Layer by clicking on the New Layer icon in the bottom left-hand corner of the Timeline.

*The key combination **Ctrl+Shift+V** can be used as a shortcut for Paste in Place.*

Paste in Place

We saw in the last chapter how Flash allows you to paste objects from the clipboard that have either been copied or cut from elsewhere within the Flash environment, or have been imported from another program.

Sometimes it is useful to copy or cut objects from different layers and paste them into another layer. Obviously it would be important to ensure that these objects are positioned exactly as they were in their original layers.

This is where **Paste in Place** comes in useful. If you copied (or cut) an object and simply pasted it into a new layer, Flash would always paste it in the centre of the Stage, ready for you to move and reposition.

However, if you go to the **Edit** menu and select **Paste in Place**, the exact positioning from the original layer will be replicated in this new layer.

Symbols and instances

7

Accessing libraries, symbols and instances

Creating symbols from graphic objects

Creating new symbols without conversion

Symbols vs objects

Changing an instance in an instant

So far we've concentrated on the creation and manipulation of static objects. However, in a short while we will start to experiment with animations, and for that we will want to use copies of our objects over and over again as we place them in different parts of the scene, or use them in different movies.

Accessing libraries, symbols and instances

Objects are stored in *libraries*, when they are then referred to as *symbols*. Each copy of the symbol used in your animation or movie is then referred to as an *instance*.

To access the library of the current movie that you are working on, you need to go to the **Window** menu and select **Library**. You can also get there by pressing **F11**. It's a good idea to anchor this panel with your others on the right-hand side of your Stage. Notice how this panel is unique in that it has three extra icons on the right-hand side (Figure 7.1). The triangle is used to sort the library contents, the square expands the window, and the rectangle contracts it again.

It is also possible to access symbols in libraries that you created for other movies. In this case you need to open up that particular library, which you do by going to the **File** menu and selecting **Open as Library** or pressing **Ctrl+Shift+O** (Figure 7.2).

Flash not only keeps a library with each and every movie you create, but it also has a collection of libraries, which it stores with its program files. When you installed Flash you will have created three libraries that you can access via **Window > Common** Libraries (Figure 7.3). They are:

When you go to the library of another movie you will not be allowed to modify its contents. Only the current library can be modified, although you are allowed to copy symbols within another library to your current library.

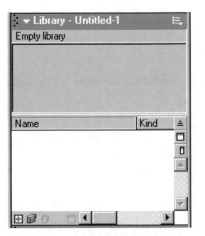

Figure 7.1 The current library panel.

Figure 7.2 Accessing the symbols in another movie library.

- Buttons;
- Learning Interactions;
- Sounds.

Opening any of these will automatically place a new panel on your collapsible panel area to the right of the Stage.

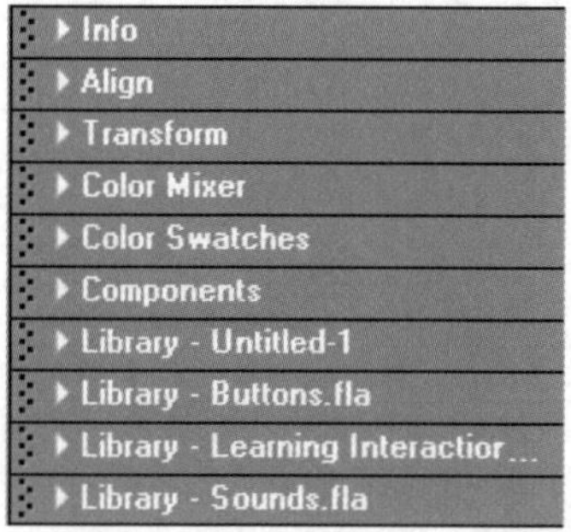

▶ Info
▶ Align
▶ Transform
▶ Color Mixer
▶ Color Swatches
▶ Components
▶ Library - Untitled-1
▶ Library - Buttons.fla
▶ Library - Learning Interactior...
▶ Library - Sounds.fla

Figure 7.3 Three libraries of symbols are provided courtesy of Flash MX.

You might find it worthwhile to create a special collection of symbols that you use repeatedly in your projects by copying them from existing movies into a special file just for this purpose.

If you were to go to the *program files* directory and look 'inside' Flash MX you would see a directory named *Libraries* hidden away in the *First Run* folder. It contains matching files of the default libraries and each is a Flash file in its own right.

When you open up a library you can view its contents in different ways and organise its contents the way it suits you – with hierarchical folders, for instance (Figure 7.4).

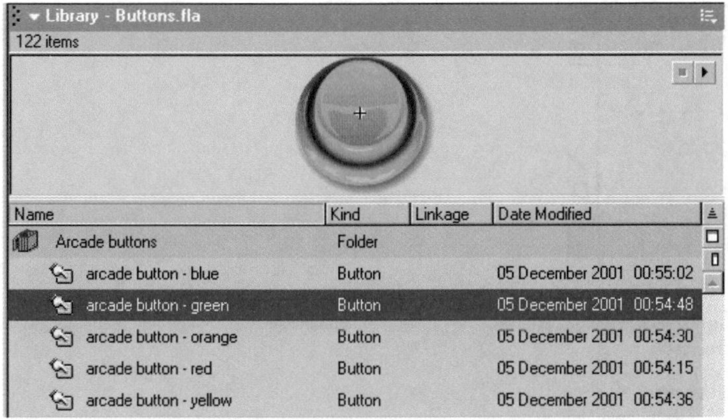

Figure 7.4 A view of the Buttons library in expanded mode.

Flash offers information on when the symbol was last modified, how many times it has been used and what type of item it is, as well as any linkages to outside graphics programs that you may have set (Figure 7.4). In expanded mode you can view the date that the symbol was last modified, the type of item it is and any linkages. The current library also shows how many times it has been used in your movie. In the contracted mode you just get to see a list of the symbols in the library.

You will also see in Figure 7.5 that the Options menu enables you to create new folders within a particular library. To add symbols to a particular folder, all you need do is drag the symbol onto the folder icon to create a hierarchy – which will prove to be especially useful when you have a library with very many symbols in it.

By default, the Use Counter does not automatically update, as it might slow down the program. However, if you go to the menu button in the top right-hand corner of the panel, you can elect either to keep the Use Counts automatically updated, or to be updated on demand (Figure 7.5).

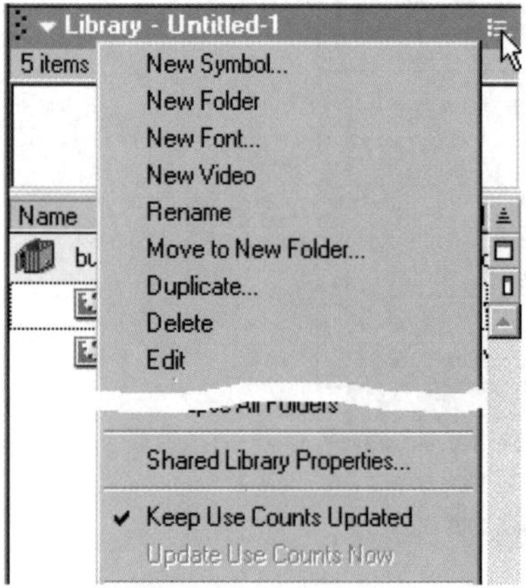

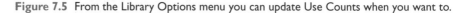

Figure 7.5 From the Library Options menu you can update Use Counts when you want to.

You will see in the current library panel that there are four icons in the bottom left-hand corner. These are, respectively:

1. New symbol;
2. New folder;
3. Symbol properties;
4. Delete item.

We'll return to items 1 and 3 in a moment. Item 2 – create new folder – is essentially the same as the *New Folder* option shown in Figure 7.5, whilst *Delete item* (also accessible from the Options menu) allows you to delete a selected library item, although a confirmation box first appears to check that you really do wish to delete the symbol since this action cannot be reversed. You can expand or close each library folder by double-clicking on it. This allows you more screen space to view the contents of other library folders.

Creating symbols from graphic objects

There will be occasions when you will wish to re-use a graphic object that you have either made or imported into Flash. By converting the graphic into a symbol you will best be able to re-use it without affecting the original in any way.

With the static object selected on your Stage go to the **Insert** menu and select **Convert to Symbol**. (You can instead press **F8**.) The Convert to Symbol dialog box will appear (Figure 7.6) which allows you to choose whether you are creating a symbol of a graphic, a button or a movie clip. It also gives it a default name based on the number of symbols already in the library, but it is usually best if you give it a name that is meaningful so that you can locate the symbol easily at a later time. You can alter the point of registration of the instance, so that your x,y coordinates are measured either from the centre or from one of the corners. There is also an **Advanced** button that sets linkages when you are coding in ActionScript, which we introduce in Chapter 11.

Once you have clicked **OK** the object on the Stage becomes an *instance* of the new symbol you have created and it is listed in your current library.

*Remember that if you delete a symbol from your library, it will also be deleted from your movie; so if you are at all in doubt, check the **Use Count** before you delete any symbols.*

You are no longer able to edit the graphic object directly on your stage once you have converted it into a symbol. Instead you have to enter symbol-editing mode (see below) to do so.

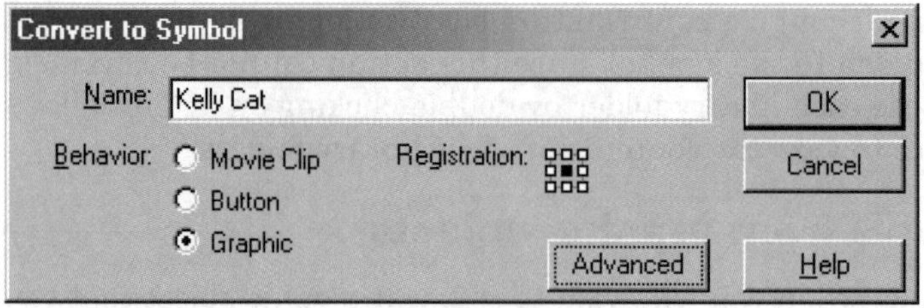

Figure 7.6 The Convert to Symbol dialog box.

Creating new symbols without conversion

If you wish to create a symbol that is to be used many times, it is not necessary to create a graphic first and then convert it to a symbol. Instead, you can create a symbol from scratch directly in **Symbol Editing** mode. Click on **New Symbol** in either the menu (Figure 7.5) or on the far left icon at the bottom of the library panel to produce a new blank symbol. This immediately puts you into symbol editing mode (shown by the new symbol flag shown in Figure 7.7 as 'Symbol 4').

You can return to the main scene by clicking on **Scene 1** (shown on the left of Figure 7.7) and if you need to return to carry out more edits on this symbol, you'll find the symbol editing entry button at the top right-hand corner of the Stage next to the percentage viewer menu, and this will bring up a drop-down list of available symbols, including your new symbol, which you can select for editing.

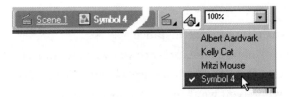

Figure 7.7 Enter Symbol Editing mode via the button at the top right-hand corner of the stage.

Symbols vs objects

At this point you might well be wondering why one should go to all the bother of using symbols when it is perfectly possible to reuse objects simply by copying them to another part of the Stage.

Well, of course you can work in that way if you want to; but by converting objects to symbols Flash only has to store the set of vector instructions for that object once. By then using multiple instances of that one symbol, Flash does not need to redefine the vector parameters each time the symbol is used. Instead it looks up its library of symbols and gleans the information from here.

You can then modify the different instances of each symbol – say, rotating it, colouring it, or whatever. But the basic set of instructions remains unaltered, and it is this that allows Flash to save a great deal of information in a nicely compact file.

You could, if you wished, skip the preview stage and simply drag the symbol name to the stage.

So, to place an instance of a symbol onto your Stage:

1. Select the layer on which you wish to place the instance.
2. Open the library containing the symbol whose instance you want to import.
3. Click once on the symbol to preview it in the upper library window (Figure 7.4).
4. Drag the preview to the Stage where you want to place your instance.
5. Release the mouse.

Changing an instance in an instant

We just mentioned that it is possible to change the appearance of an instance without altering the original symbol. In particular we can:

1. scale it;
2. skew it;
3. rotate it;
4. change its colour;
5. change its transparency.

Scaling, skewing and rotation is carried out in exactly the same way as you would scale, skew or rotate any other object (see Chapter 3); but you alter the colour and transparency by calling up the **Properties** dialog box below the Stage. Click on the drop-down menu labelled **Color** and you will be offered a choice of the following:

- Brightness;
- Tint;
- Alpha;
- Advanced.

If we decided to alter the brightness of one of a pair of instances, for instance, we would select **Brightness** from the drop-down menu. The amount of brightness can be altered either by tweaking the slider tab or by entering an amount directly into the brightness value box.

Similarly, we can change the colour balance by selecting **Tint** from the drop-down menu. Here we can not only choose the colour we want – either by keying in values to the RGB boxes, or by clicking on the colour grid – but also set the degree of tinting to be applied to the instance – again, by using either the slider control or by entering an exact amount (Figure 7.8).

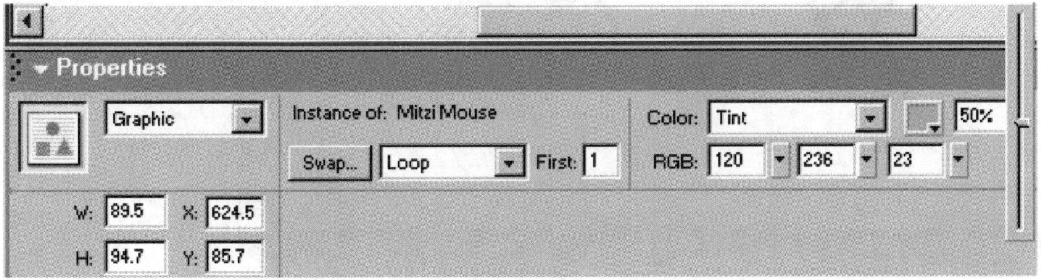

Figure 7.8 Tweaking the Tint properties of an instance.

If we want to alter the transparency of the instance we change its **Alpha** setting. A 100% setting makes it completely opaque; a 0% setting sets it transparent. Once again we can use either the slider or enter a number directly into the Alpha box.

Flash MX also allows you to change a symbol instance's colour and transparency simultaneously. For this, you need to select **Advanced** from that drop-down menu. In Figure 7.9 you can see that each of the colour and alpha channels have two sliders. This may at first cause some confusion. Basically the left and right sliders have different jobs to do. The *left* sliders cause changes in the values of the original colour balance whilst the *right* sliders add colour or opacity to the entire object.

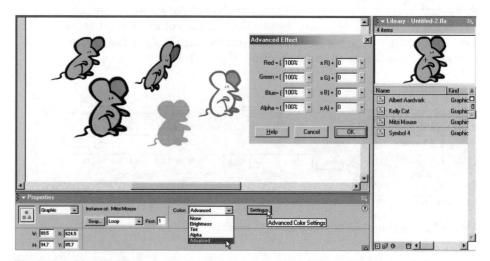

Figure 7.9 Altering different instances of the same symbol using Advanced Color Settings.

Imagine, for instance, that you have three circles within your instance. One is coloured pure red (i.e. it has an RGB value of 255,0,0), another is pure green, whilst the third is pure blue.

If you reduce the value of the left-hand menu, it will reduce the amount of blue in the blue circle, but will have no effect on the green or red circles since they have no blue element within them. However, if you increase the right-hand blue element, it adds blue to everything, including both the red and green circles, and these will now start to change colour.

As is usual, a little experimentation will soon make this clear.

Sometime you might want to swap over one instance for another after you have made changes to its size, rotation, colour, or whatever. Flash MX makes this easy. Having made any modifications to the original instance, open up the **Properties** dialog box below the Stage.

Now click on the **Swap** button to open up the Swap Symbol dialog box, choose an alternative symbol and click **OK** (Figure 7.10).

Finally, there may be occasions when you want to break the link between an instance of a particular symbol and the symbol itself. For instance, you might wish to change the shape of a symbol in certain instances, but not in others.

The best way to do this is to select the instance of the symbol whose link you want to break. Then from the **Modify** menu select **Break Apart** (or **Ctrl+B**).

You can then alter the shape (or whatever) of this object and even save it once more as a new symbol if you are likely to need this new shape again.

Remember that when you edit a symbol, rather than an instance, it will not only change the symbol that resides in your library, but also every instance of the symbol within your movie.

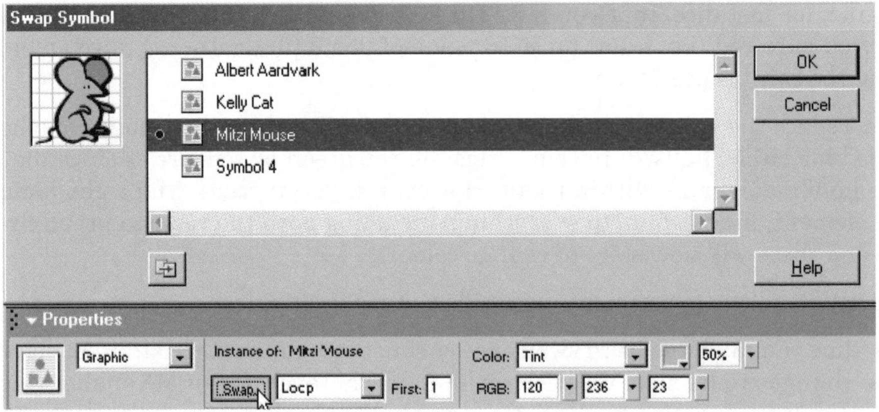

Figure 7.10 Using the Swap option in the definition section of the Properties dialog box.

Animation 8

Animation basics

Frame types

Making a simple animation

Motion Tweening

Moving objects along a predefined path

Shape Tweening

Shape tweening multiple objects

Using shape hints to improve your morphing

Getting shape tweens to move along a path

Reversing frames

Animated masks

Saving animations

A note about scenes

For obvious reasons, we have so far taken up over half this book looking at the basics of using Flash. However, it is only when we move on to the use of animations that Flash really starts to come into its own. It is, after all, probably one of the main reasons that you bought the software in the first place.

Animation basics

In Flash you can:

- move an object across the Stage;
- increase or decrease its size;
- rotate the object;
- change its colour;
- change its basic shape;
- make it fade in or fade out.

There are two basic methods one can use in creating a Flash animation:

1. Make frames individually.
2. Create starting and ending frames and let Flash 'tween' between them.

If you look at the Timeline you will see that there are very many cells, or **frames** within your movie. Assuming you have a totally blank Flash Stage, you will see that all the frames look blank apart from the first which has a small open bullet in it.

Figure 8.1 At the start of a new movie, all the frames in the Timeline look blank.

Frame types

Whenever you place an object within the Timeline of a movie, you have to create a **keyframe**. Normally you would leave some of the frames blank between the first keyframe and the next keyframe – we'll see why in a moment. Let's insert a keyframe into frame 5. Click once on frame 5 and then use the **Insert** menu (or right-click on it) to turn it into a keyframe. The latter is much quicker and easier! Straight away, the frame divisions before frame 5 disappear, and a vertical line is placed before the keyframe (Figure 8.2) which also contains an outline bullet.

Let's now place an object – say, a circle – onto the Stage at this frame. Straight away the bullet is made solid in the keyframe to show it is no longer empty (Figure 8.3).

Next, let's insert a blank keyframe into frame 10. Remember that you can:

- right-click on the frame and select **Blank Keyframe**;
- go to your **Insert** menu and select **Blank Keyframe**;
- click once on the frame and press **F7**.

*Another way of creating a keyframe is to use the **F6** function key which converts an ordinary frame into a keyframe.*

Figure 8.2 Inserting a keyframe at frame 5 places a vertical line in front of it.

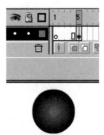

Figure 8.3 A blob in a keyframe shows it is no longer empty.

You'll notice that the Stage area is blank. The circle has disappeared. You'll also see that a small vertical rectangle is placed just before frame 10 (just as appeared in frame 4 when we created a new keyframe in frame 5), and that the frames between 5 and 10 inclusive have turned grey (Figure 8.4).

If we click on any frame between 5 and 10 – i.e. in the greyed-out frames – we will continue to see the circle on the Stage area (Figure 8.5). In effect, the blank frame has deleted everything from sight from Frame 10 onwards. The clear rectangle is a marker to show that the frame is an end mark for whatever came before.

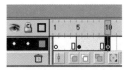

Figure 8.4 Inserting a blank keyframe adds a small rectangle just before it.

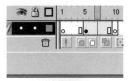

Figure 8.5 We have placed a filled circle in frame 5 (note the solid bullet), so clicking on Frame 7 will continue to show the circle. Note the rectangles in frames 4 and 9!

You can alter the size with which you view the Timeline in order to see more or fewer frames. This could be useful when your Timeline starts to get filled up. Go to the **Frame View** pop-up menu to the top right of the Stage and select an option (Figure 8.6).

So far we have had the option of adding either:

1. a Blank Keyframe;
2. a Keyframe.

Although Flash talks about 'inserting' keyframes, it actually does nothing of the sort! What it really does is to convert an existing frame into a keyframe. The number of frames remains constant. If instead you use the **Insert Frame** command, then Flash does, indeed, add extra frames.

You can also copy or paste frames by using the keyboard with **Ctrl + Alt + C** or **Ctrl + Alt + V** as appropriate.

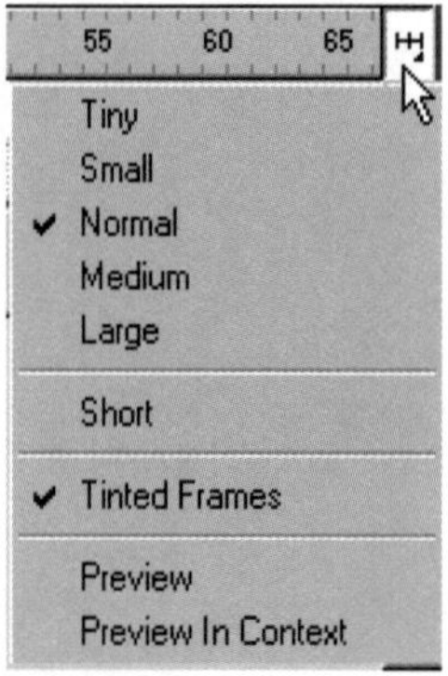

Figure 8.6 Select the Timeline size from the Frame View pop-up menu.

If you wish to change the contents of the scene completely, then go for option 1. If you intend solely to make minor changes, then plump for option 2. The latter duplicates whatever has gone before, allowing you to add objects, move things around, or whatever else you like.

You may quite often find the need to insert extra frames – and a quick way to do this, apart from laboriously inserting single frames, is to copy and paste empty frames from the end of the Timeline into the point in the Timeline you wish to expand. However, you cannot simply copy and paste using the normal Windows shortcuts, otherwise you will paste over whatever frames are already in existence. Instead, right-click on your selected number of empty frames and select **Copy Frames** or **Paste Frames** as appropriate.

Just as there are two commands for inserting frames – depending on whether you really do wish to add an extra frame, rather than a keyframe – so, too, are there two commands (confusingly contained in the **Insert** menu!) for removing frames:

1. **Clear Keyframe**;
2. **Remove Frame**.

The former simply removes the keyframe status from your selected frame. It does not remove it from the Timeline. The latter, on the other hand, deletes the frame entirely from your movie and reduces the number of frames accordingly.

Making a simple animation

Let's kick off by creating an extremely simple animation using frame-by-frame animation. Open up a new Flash document and switch on the grid (**View > Grid > Show Grid**) for ease of accurate placing. Select the first frame and draw a circle on the Stage.

Next, click on the second frame and insert a keyframe as described above. Immediately, two things happen: a bullet is added to show that frame 2 is now a keyframe, and the circle you drew before becomes selected. Drag the selected circle to a new position a few centimetres to the right. Repeat once more with the third frame (see Figure 8.7).

If you now click frames 1, 2 and 3 in turn you will see the circle 'move' to its new positions. However, to see your movie automatically, go to the **Control** menu and select **Play**. It's all over pretty quickly, but if instead you go to **Control > Loop Playback** and then **Play** the scene again it will continue looping through your movie.

Sometimes, when you try to remove a keyframe it appears that Flash refuses to carry out your instructions. This is most likely to happen if you try to remove a keyframe without deleting the contents of the in-between frames that have picked up their information from the keyframe you are trying to remove. In its attempt to make sense of your conflicting instructions, Flash creates a virtual keyframe. The result is that you end up trying to delete a keyframe, which Flash replaces with an identical one! Instead, select all the associated in-between frames with your keyframe and delete the lot in one go.

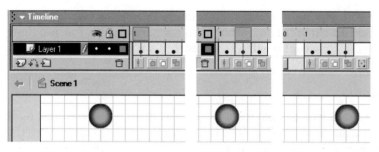

Figure 8.7 Using insert keyframe commands to duplicate and move the circle.

Smoothing an animation

If you want to smooth the jerky animation you just created it is necessary to insert more keyframes into the animation and reposition the circle with smaller movements. It means that the final file size will be greater, of course, but you need to strike a happy balance between smoother motion and keeping the file size to a minimum.

Between frames 1 and 2, and frames 2 and 3, choose **Insert Frames** from the **Insert** menu and nudge the circle along for each extra frame. Now when you preview your movie the action should be smoother, but it will probably still appear jerky. What can we do next?

Well, maybe part of the problem lies in the fact that the circle is not moving equidistantly between each keyframe. To help with the accurate placing of each circle let's use Flash's *Onion Skinning* facility. This is turned on by clicking on the button, shown in Figure 8.8. Now you can see the contents of each

You can step through the frames sequentially by clicking on the '<' or '>' keys repeatedly.

keyframe at once. However, you cannot edit the dimmed circles except by selecting their individual keyframes, when that particular dimmed circle will become full-colour.

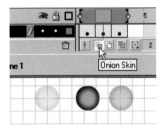

Figure 8.8 Turning on the Onion Skin feature allows you to see all keyframes at once.

If you click on the button to the immediate right of the Onion Skin button the dimmed objects will become outlines only, allowing you to judge placing over-lapping objects more accurately (Figure 8.9).

If you are not able to see as many 'onion skins' as you were expecting, click on the **Modify Onion Markers** button (Figure 8.10) and select the option of viewing 2, 5 or All the frames.

Alternatively, drag the onion skin markers shown as brackets around your keyframes at the top of the Timeline (see Figure 8.11).

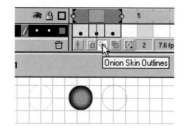

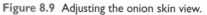

Figure 8.9 Adjusting the onion skin view.

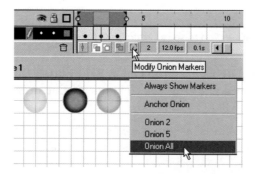

Figure 8.10 You can choose how many 'onions' you view from this menu.

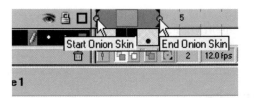

Figure 8.11 You can drag the onion skin outer markers to view more or fewer skins.

Editing Multiple Frames

It may well be that, having created your animation frames, you want to reposition one of your animated objects. You could, in theory, move each individual instance of your object and realign them using the grid. A much better option is to use the **Edit Multiple Frames** option that you can switch on by using the button two to the right of the Onion Skin button (Figure 8.12). By turning on this option you can effectively edit objects in different keyframes simultaneously.

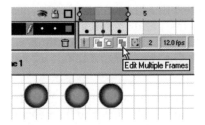

Figure 8.12 Edit a number of frames together with the Multiple Frame option.

Once you choose the Edit Multiple Frames option, onion skinning no longer works, since you have effectively chosen to edit each keyframe instance at once.

Having clicked this button, select the arrow tool in the toolbar and drag a rectangle around all the instances of the circle on your Stage. Each of the circles is selected. Now go to the **Align** panel to get each of the circles lined up with one another (Figure 8.13).

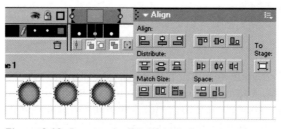

Figure 8.13 By using the Edit Multiple Frames option you can align and space each object instances.

Setting the Frame Rate

Flash allows you to set the frame rate which determines how many frames are displayed every second. Set the frame rate too fast, and the movie will rush past in a blur. Too slow, and the animation will be jerky. Normally, the standard rate for a feature film is 24 frames per second. On the web, 12 fps is a good rate. By default, Flash sets the frame rate at 12 fps.

To change the default setting, which affects the entire movie, go to the **Modify** menu and select **Document**. Alternatively you can double click the frame rate value at the bottom of the Timeline. The **Document Properties** dialog box appears (Figure 8.14).

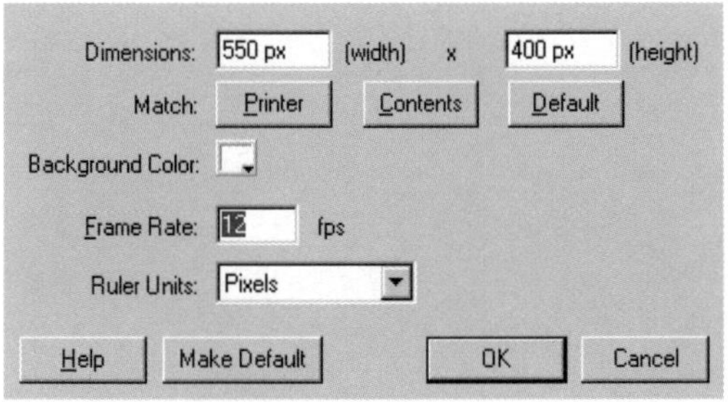

Figure 8.14 Setting the frame rate in the Document Properties dialog box.

Although the frame rate of a movie remains constant, you can speed up or slow down a particular section of a movie by adding or deleting frames from that section. Inserting in-between frames adds very little to the overall file size, but if you add extra keyframes in order to show the object in a slightly different position each time, the overall movie file will increase in size considerably.

Motion tweening

Frame-by-frame animation has two major drawbacks associated with it. On the one hand it is extremely time consuming, and it also creates very large files. By using **tweening**, Flash gets round both of these problems.

Tweening comes in two forms:

1. Motion tweening;
2. Shape tweening.

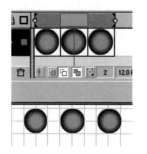

We saw in Figure 8.6 that it is possible to increase the size of the frame representations within the timeline. From that same drop-down menu you can also select either **Preview** or **Preview in Context**, which will give you previews of your individual frames either at full size or in relation to one another (Figure 8.15).

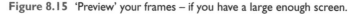

Figure 8.15 'Preview' your frames – if you have a large enough screen.

By defining the beginning and end keyframes, Flash creates a series of frames with incremental changes that change the first keyframe to the last keyframe, morphing from one to the other.

Let's create a simple motion tween to move a circle from the left of our Stage to the right. Firstly, create a new movie and, in keyframe 1, add a circle to the Stage. With frame 1 still selected, select **Create Motion Tween** from the **Insert** menu, or right-click on the frame and select it from the menu. Look in your local Library where you will see that the circle is made into a symbol, which Flash calls, by default, 'Tween 1'. Now select frame 10 and **Insert > Frame**. A dotted line appears in the Timeline showing there is an unresolved tween operation. Convert frame 10 to a keyframe, however, and the tween information thinks it is complete. The dotted line turns into an arrow (Figure 8.16).

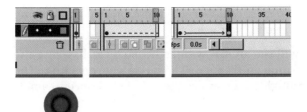

Figure 8.16 Creating a motion tween.

However, so far nothing has changed. Select the circle in frame 10 and move it to a new position and now, when you **Play** the animation (or press **Enter**), the circle moves smoothly from one side to the other.

You can view the tweening that has been created by looking at the individual frames with the onion skinning turned on (Figure 8.17).

The word 'tweening' is derived from the action of creating in-between frames, which is what cartoon animators used to do laboriously by hand when creating cartoon feature films.

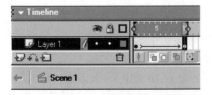

Figure 8.17 Viewing the motion tween with onion skins showing.

You can add extra keyframes into an already-created motion tween, allowing you to alter the path of the animation if you want to.

If you look at Figure 8.17 you will see an arrow links frame 0 to 10. Using the right-click menu, insert a keyframe on frame 6. The circle appropriate to the tween position at frame 6 is highlighted. Now, drag the circle instance to a new position and let go (Figure 8.18).

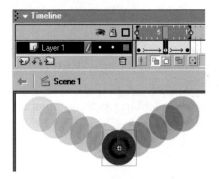

Figure 8.18 Inserting an extra keyframe into a motion tween.

Now when you play your animation, the redefined path will be substituted for your original path.

Tweening colour changes and fading in and out

As well as using Motion Tween to move objects around the Stage, you can also use it to change the colours of objects, or even to fade an object in and out of the picture. Let's start a new project and create a coloured square in frame 1. You can only motion-tween grouped objects or symbols, so we first convert this square into a symbol by clicking on **Insert > Convert to Symbol**. (Give the symbol a name in the dialog box that appears such as 'square'.)

In the Timeline we next create a new keyframe at, say, frame 10. With keyframe 10 still selected, go to the **Properties** panel below your Stage and select **Color > Tint**. This allows us to select a new colour for our square (Figure 8.19) and also how much (what percentage) of tint to apply to the object. In other words, if you leave the percentage setting at 50% you will get an even mixture of the first and second colours. But if you want your square to turn completely to the second colour, set your tint percentage at 100%.

If, instead of changing colour, you wish to fade out the object, choose **Alpha** from the drop-down menu. The Alpha setting determines the transparency of your object. A zero-value effectively washes your object completely from the picture.

Go to the first frame and create a motion tween using the **Insert** menu. Finally you can test your colour change by playing your animation in the normal way.

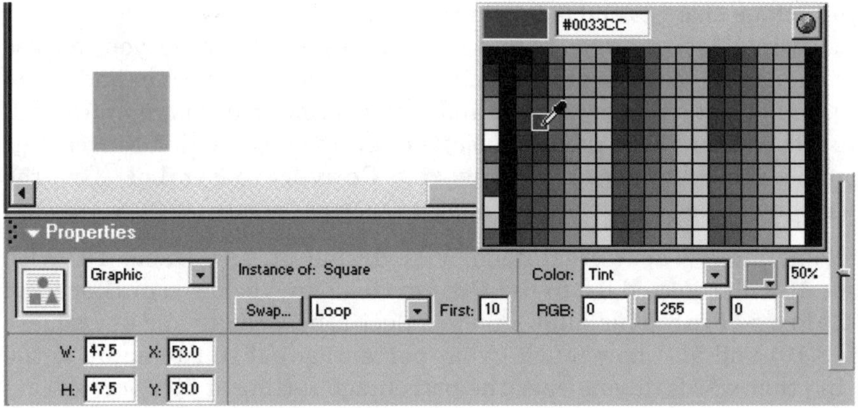

Figure 8.19 Changing the colour of the instance.

Tweening objects that change size

Not only can you create a motion tween that moves your object and changes colour, but you can also change its size as well. In your final keyframe resize the instance, but before you try out your animation, look in the **Properties** panel and ensure that the checkbox labelled **Scale** is selected (Figure 8.20). If it is not, the square will stay the same size until the last frame and then suddenly expand for just that one frame transition.

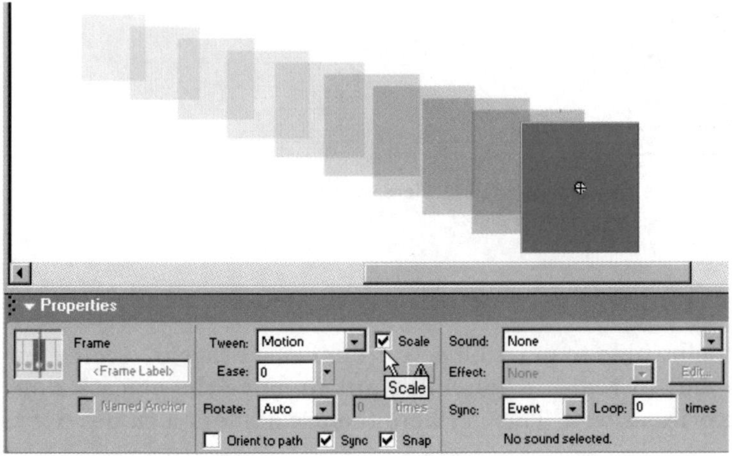

Figure 8.20 Onion skins show a motion tween for an object that changes size as it moves.

Rotating objects

If you want to rotate an object as part of your motion tween, you need to give more information than just two keyframes can offer. If you think about it, an object could rotate clockwise or anti-clockwise, or even flip it over. Flash allows you to define the method of rotation by bringing up that same **Properties** panel we used just a moment ago (Figure 8.21). You can slow down the rotation at the start or end of the spin by changing the value of the **Ease** box, depending on whether you want to 'ease in' or 'ease out'. The **Rotation Options** menu allows you to determine whether rotation should be clockwise or anti-clockwise.

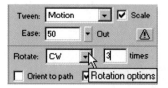

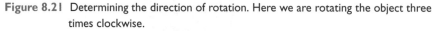

Figure 8.21 Determining the direction of rotation. Here we are rotating the object three times clockwise.

Moving objects along a predefined path

It's all very well being able to move objects around the Stage in a collection of straight lines, but in real life you will want to move the objects along curves and trajectories as well. This is where the use of motion guides comes into its own.

Motion guides define the paths for a tweened object to move along. Each guide has to be created on a separate layer, but you can use one guide to control a number of objects on different layers.

Let's start off a new Flash document and place a rectangular object in the first frame. Convert it into a symbol (**Insert > Convert to Symbol**) and then create a motion tween to frame 20. At the bottom of the Timeline we next click the **Add Motion Guide** button (Figure 8.22), which adds a new layer directly above the layer you selected. The layer you were working on is now indented under the Guide layer.

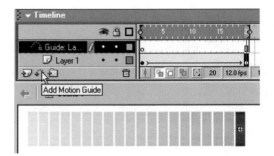

Figure 8.22 Add a Motion Guide layer.

Once you have selected this guide layer you can now draw the path you want your object to follow by using the pencil tool, oval, rectangle, line or brush. In the Properties dialog box ensure the **Snap** checkbox is ticked and then tweak the start and end objects directly over the ends of the motion path you have just defined. Although the motion path is visible at the present time (Figure 8.23), it will not be shown in the final movie.

In Figure 8.23 you can see that the object – although it slavishly follows the motion path – remains at its original angle. But in normal motion you would expect the object to twist and turn in sympathy with the direction of movement.

This time, therefore, click on one of the frames in Layer 1 and ensure that the **Orient to path** checkbox shown in Figure 8.21 is checked. The object should now always face the direction of movement (Figure 8.24).

It's a good idea, once you have created your motion path, to lock this layer so that you cannot alter it accidentally.

If you have sudden changes of direction in your motion guide, such as in Figure 8.24, Flash may have difficulty in aligning the object at every frame. If your moving object looks as if it needs a bit of help, there is nothing to stop you inserting an extra keyframe or two and manually altering the direction it faces.

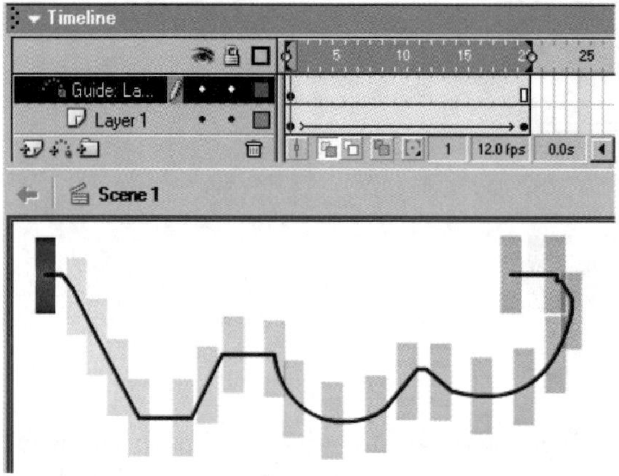

Figure 8.23 The object follows the defined motion path.

Shape tweening

Just as you can tween objects to make them move from one part of the Stage to another, so too can you get an object to morph into another. This type of tweening is called **shape tweening**.

Just as in motion tweening, shape tweening requires you to define the beginning and end shape; Flash then creates the in-between frames morphing one shape gradually into the next.

Timeline
Guide: La...
Layer 1
5
10
15
20
25
1
12.0 fps
0.0s
Scene 1

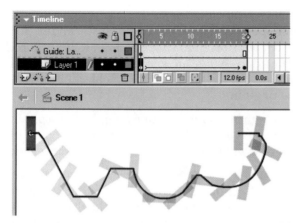

Figure 8.24 The object now rotates in the direction of movement.

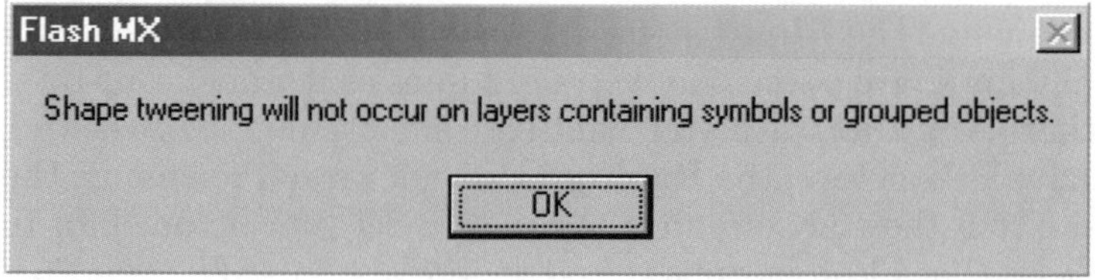

Flash MX
Shape tweening will not occur on layers containing symbols or grouped objects.
OK

Figure 8.25 Flash warns you if you try to shape tween the wrong type of object.

There are some functions that shape tweening can do that can also be carried out in motion tweening. The shape that you wish to tween to might, for instance, be a different colour from your original shape. It follows, therefore, that shape tweening can be instructed to change an object's colour as well as its size and location. You cannot, however, get Flash to rotate an object or move it along a motion guide using shape tweening.

Let's start by transforming a circle into a square – an example of morphing simple lines and fills. We'll create a new Flash document and draw a circle in frame 1. For ease of demonstration we will make the circle in outline form only, although we could just as easily have made it filled.

Next we select frame 10 in the Timeline, but this time we'll **Insert** a **Blank Keyframe** which has the effect of removing everything from the Stage at this particular frame. Now we can create a square on the Stage. Don't worry about the exact placing of the square right now. We can worry about that later.

Select frame 1 once more, and in the **Properties** panel select **Shape** from the **Tweens** drop-down menu. The **Blend** menu allows you to choose whether you want Flash to retain any sharp corners and straight lines as it transforms from one shape to another (**Angular**) or if you want it to smooth out the tweening shapes (**Distributive**). As before, the **Easing** value allows you to change the transition speed at either the start or end of the tween. Set your onion skins to visible and you will see that Flash morphs the circle into a square (Figure 8.26).

On the Timeline, if we have Tinted Frames active (which is set in the pop-up menu at the end of the Timeline – see Figure 8.6) then Flash turns the frames containing the shape tween light green.

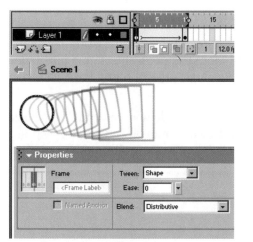

Figure 8.26 Shape tweening in action.

The onion skinning shows clearly that the circle and square are not aligned. By choosing either frame 1 or frame 10 we can nudge the circle or square one on top of the other so that they are perfectly aligned (Figure 8.27).

Figure 8.27 At last the circle and square are perfectly aligned.

Shape tweening multiple objects

Because Flash would have difficulty in determining which starting shape morphs to which ending shape if you had more than one object on a particular layer, it is advisable to restrict yourself to a single object on any layer you wish to shape-tween.

This is best illustrated if we attempt to create the following morph. We'll place a square and circle on one layer and ask Flash to morph to the same square and circle, but placed in a different area of the Stage. We'll make sure their respective paths cross over (Figure 8.28).

Figure 8.28 The circle and square are set diametrically oposite one another prior to tweening.

As you can see from Figure 8.29, Flash has chosen to morph the square into the circle and vice versa in preference to crossing their morphing paths.

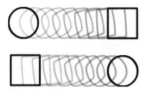

Figure 8.29 The circle and square have morphed into one another in preference to crossing over.

Using shape hints to improve your morphing

When we transformed a circle into a square it was fairly obvious how Flash would morph the shape. Sometimes, however, especially with complicated shapes, Flash has difficulty in interpreting exactly what you want it to do. You can help it by providing **Shape Hints**.

Say that you wanted to morph the raccoon in Figure 8.30 into a pig. Obviously you will have to provide your own images to try this out. But remember, as you cannot shape-tween symbols or grouped objects we have first to break them apart using the **Modify** menu.

Figure 8.30 Preparing to morph a racoon into a pig.

If you think you have made a mistake with the placing of your shape hints, you can reposition them at any time you want. Alternatively, you can remove a shape hint by clicking on the initial keyframe and then dragging the hint off the Stage.

We begin by placing the raccoon in frame 1 and inserting a blank keyframe in frame 10 where the pig is then placed. Select frame 1 again and in the **Properties** panel ask it to shape-tween from one animal to the other.

With frame 1 still selected, go to your **Modify** menu and choose **Shape > Add Shape Hint** or – far quicker – press **Ctrl + Shift + H**. A little red spot appears in the centre of the raccoon, which is exactly duplicated in the centre of the pig image when you move across to frame 10. This red spot marks your first shape hint's position. Unlike the way in which some morphing programs work, it is important in Flash to place shape hints in order (either clockwise or anti-clockwise) around the edge of the object. So drag the red spot, say, to the end of the raccoon's tail and then, in frame 10 drag the red spot to the end of the pig's tail.

Continue to place shape hints around the edge of each animal (Figure 8.31) so that Flash is given help in determining which parts of the animals should morph to their respective mouse parts.

Figure 8.31 Six shape hints have been added to help with the morph.

Getting shape tweens to move along a path

We've already said that you cannot use shape tweening to move an object along a guide path. So what do you do if you want a circle, say, to turn into a square, but to move along a loop as it does so?

The answer is to use a combination of shape tweening and motion tweening.

As we did before, create a shape-tween to morph a circle into a square. Let's do it over 20 frames, so that the last keyframe is defined as frame 20. Now select all 20 frames in the tween sequence and, using the **Insert** menu convert all 20 frames to keyframes.

Flash keeps the tween information within each keyframe that you have just created. As Flash allows you to place any keyframe object where you want to, it is a simple matter to drag each instance to a position on the Stage. To get more accuracy, you could create a new guide layer and draw a curved line on it. Go to the **View > Guides** menu and select **Snap to Guides**. Now when you drag the object close to the guideline it should snap into place against the line.

Reversing frames

Sometimes a seemingly complex animation can be made much simpler by reversing a sequence of some of your frames. For instance, if an object grows and then shrinks, then why not save yourself time and effort by creating the growth sector and then simply copying and reversing these frames for the second part of the animation.

Flash can do this very easily. In your Timeline, select the frames you want to copy by highlighting them and then selecting **Copy Frames** from the **Edit** menu.

Now paste these frames into position immediately behind the frames you have created using the same menu. Your animation now contains two growth animations, one immediately following the other. Select the second set of frames that you have just pasted and from your **Modify** menu, select **Frames > Reverse**. Flash reverses the order of the second set of frames creating the illusion of an object growing and then contracting.

Animated tasks

We learned in Chapter 6 that you could selectively hide or reveal objects by using mask layers. There is no reason why that mask should not, in itself, be a moving object. You can use any of the three types of tweening – motion tweening, shape tweening or frame-by-frame animation – to create a moving mask.

For instance, if we wanted some text to be revealed by a 'spotlight' over time, we could make a mask that contained a solid circle which was motion-tweened across the Stage. Any text in the associated masked layer would then automatically be revealed as the circle moved over it. Let's try it out.

The first thing, then, is to add some text somewhere on the Stage and then to fill the following frames by inserting a keyframe at, say, frame 30. Now create a mask layer and in frame 1 of this mask layer place a solid circle over the start of the text. Remember that you will need to unlock the mask layer in order to be able to edit it!

Next we create a motion tween along the mask layer such that the circle ends up at the right hand end of the text at the end of the tween process. If we turn on Onion Skin view we can see that a series of circles runs along the text (Figure 8.32).

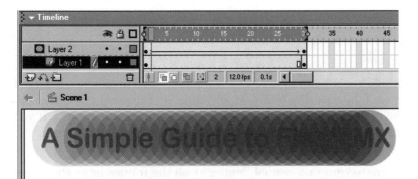

Figure 8.32 We add some text to the Stage, add a mask layer and add a circle.

Remember that any solid area in the mask layer allows us to see to the layer below; any clear area in the mask hides the area below. The effect, when you run **Control > Test Movie**, is text that is sequentially highlighted by a moving circle. Very impressive output for very little work!

Saving animations

So, we've created our tweened image and we could, if we wanted, simply save it along with the rest of the movie. However, we've already seen that if it is at all possible that the same sequence could be reused, it will take up much less memory if we save this moving sequence as a graphic symbol in its own right and then reuse the graphic symbol from our library.

Flash allows us to save moving images in one of two ways:

1. animated graphic symbol;
2. movie clip symbol.

Animated symbols are unable to save any soundtracks or interactive features (both of which we'll be covering later). Movie clips, on the other hand are self-contained and can be positioned in just one frame of your movie frames. If you are likely to want to edit an instance of your animation when it is reused, you should save it as an animated symbol.

To create an animated graphic symbol, highlight all the frames in all the layers you want to save and choose **Edit > Copy Frames**. Next, create a new symbol by selecting **Insert > New Symbol**. From the resulting **Properties** dialog box choose **Graphic**.

Once you click on **OK** a new symbol is created in the library, but it has just one frame and one Timeline. In frame 1 use **Edit > Paste Frames** to copy the animation frames into their own new symbol.

Remember when you come to use the animated symbol later on to allow enough frames to contain the entire symbol clip, unless, of course, you want to have overlapping Timelines to allow simultaneous actions.

To create a movie clip symbol, you do exactly the same as before when saving an animated symbol, except that you choose **Movie Clip** rather than **Graphic** in the Symbol Properties dialog box. Movie clips have their own Timeline and will play continuously until such time as a new blank keyframe is placed within that Timeline to stop the movie running. Unlike animated graphic symbols,

*The only clue given that a library symbol is actually an animated symbol is by looking in the top right hand corner of the library panel. An animated symbol has **Stop** and **Play** buttons showing, with which you can preview your animation.*

movie clips need to be exported to a test mode before they can be viewed. This is simple enough, however. From the **Control** menu choose either **Test Movie** or **Test Scene** to get Flash to export the movie clip to a shockwave format (.swf) file which it will then display.

A note about scenes

Creating a movie with 10 or 20 frames is easy enough to handle; but what happens if your final movie runs to hundreds of frames? You could, in theory, scroll backwards and forwards along the Timeline finding the relevant bits of your movie. It's much easier, however, to break the movie up into manageable-sized chunks called **Scenes**.

You can create scenes and arrange the order in which they play by opening **Window > Scene** which you can dock on your right hand collection of panels if you want to. Rearrange their order simply by dragging one above the other (Figure 8.33).

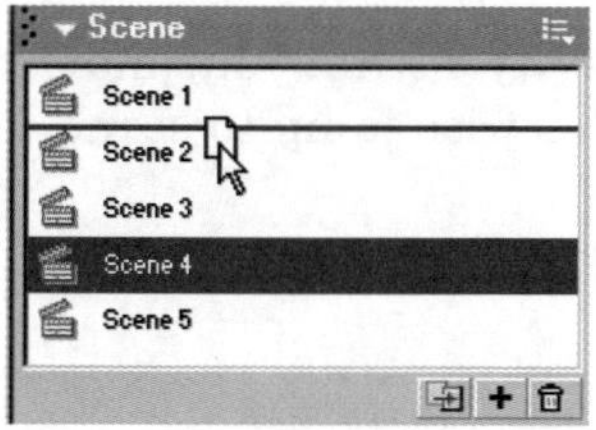

Figure 8.33 The Scene inspector window.

Once Flash has finished with one scene it automatically starts playing the next one. It follows, therefore, that in order to maintain continuity between scenes it is a good idea to copy the entire contents of each layer of the last frame of your current scene to the beginning frame of the next scene in order to ensure the accurate placing of any elements on the Stage.

You can tell at a glance which scene you are currently editing by the flag that comes up to the left of the Timeline – as in Figure 8.34.

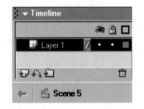

Figure 8.34 Flash leaves you in no doubt as to which scenes you are currently editing.

Scenes are particularly useful when using interactivity within your movie: 'If such an event happens then jump to scene 5; otherwise jump to scene 7' for instance.

Interactivity

Action types

Frame actions

Frame labels, comments and anchors

Some basic actions

Buttons

Interactivity with buttons

You'll save yourself time and eyestrain if you assign action frames to one layer of your Timeline only. That way, when you are searching for an action frame in the middle of a long movie it will be much easier to find it. Name the layer 'Actions' and lock it so that you cannot assign objects to it by accident.

So far we've been concentrating on sequential animation – where Flash moves from one scene to the next, for instance. However, there is no reason why you cannot instruct Flash to move from the end of one sequence to the start of another, or from any point in a scene to any other scene or frame you wish.

You give instructions to Flash by assigning actions to frames and buttons. A frame with an action assigned to it has an 'a' displayed within the Timeline (see Figure 9.1).

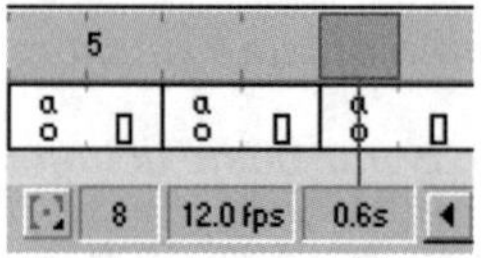

Figure 9.1 An 'a' is displayed in keyframes containing actions.

Action types

There are two types of basic Action in Flash:

1. Frame Actions;
2. Button Actions.

The first refers to actions that need no user input to generate the action. When the movie reaches a particular action frame in its playback it carries out the instruction. Individual frames can each contain many actions. A button action, on the other hand, requires input from the user before it carries out the instruction.

Frame actions

An action is assigned to a frame from the **Actions – Frame** panel, accessed as usual by **right-clicking** on the frame and selecting **Actions** (Figure 9.2).

Figure 9.2 Actions are added from the Frame Actions dialog box.

By clicking on one of the action classes, you can bring up a menu of available commands (Figure 9.3).

We'll look at these actions in more detail later on. But once you have selected a keyframe, double-clicking on any one of these actions will copy it to the right hand panel and bring up a parameters box just above it (Figure 9.4).

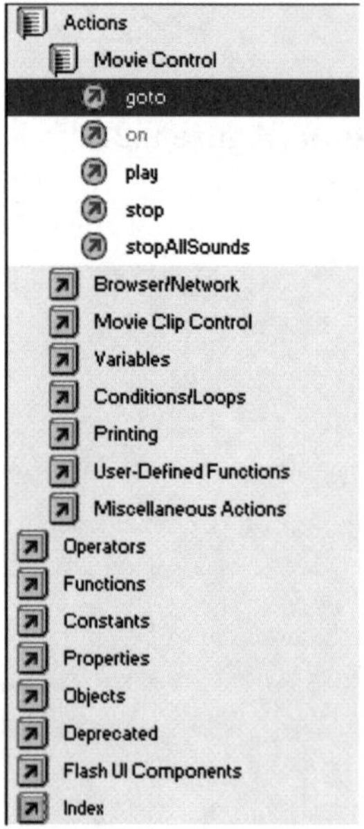

Figure 9.3 Bringing up the Actions menu.

You can keep on adding actions to this one frame so that you could, for example, turn on anti-aliasing to improve the quality of the playback, stop all sounds which might still be playing from previous instructions and then jump to another frame. You can remove previously inserted actions by highlighting the particular action and then clicking on the '-' button.

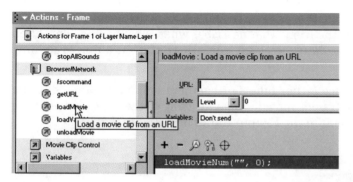

Figure 9.4 The parameters for the action appear above the listed action.

Note on the right hand side of the actions list that there are up and down buttons. These let you alter the order in which the actions are carried out. Flash always starts from the top of the list and works its way downwards. So, for instance, if there were two instructions – one of which took you to another frame and the second of which took you to a new URL (Uniform Resource Locator or, more simply, Web page address), then if the former were at the top of the list you would always be taken to the new frame, whilst if the latter headed up the action list you would always be redirected to the new URL.

Frame labels, comments and anchors

Although you can easily tell Flash to jump to a particular frame from one of your action frames, it is often better (especially in longer movies) to give your target frame a label and to instruct Flash to jump to the label rather than the frame number. If you were to insert or delete frames after specifying a frame number you might have to redefine your jumps, so the use of labels obviates this.

Sometimes, too, for frames that are not the targets of action frames, it is useful to add comments about the frame that describes what is happening. This often makes it easier at a later date to pick up from where you left off programming the movie.

Flash allows you to place either labels or comments on any frame, but you cannot add both to one frame. You add them by going to the **Properties** dialog box and inserting a label into the **Frame Label** box (Figure 9.5).

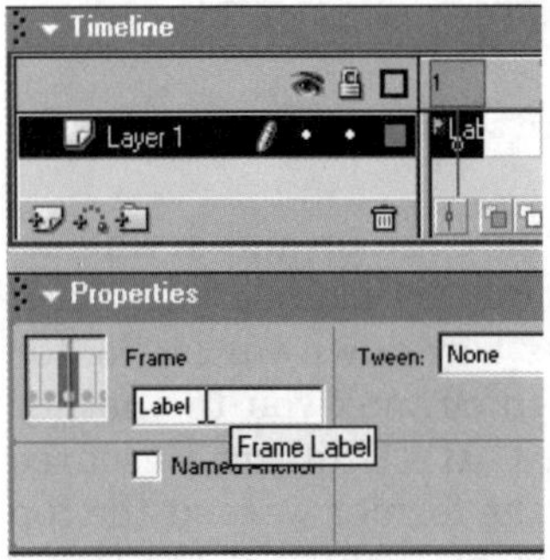

Figure 9.5 Add labels via the Properties Frame Label box.

You add a comment in exactly the same way, but precede your text with two slashes ('//') – as shown in Figure 9.6.

When you add a label, the Timeline will add a little red flag to the frame and display as much of the label as it can. A comment will instead have the effect of adding two green slashes as well as the comment to the Timeline representation.

Sometimes, however, there may not be room to see the entire comment or label because of a following keyframe, but as you can see in Figure 9.6, you can always see a 'tool tip' associated with a label or comment when you hover over the Timeline frame.

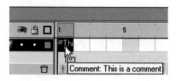

Figure 9.6 A comment begins with two slashes.

There is another type of label known as a **Named Anchor**. In Figure 9.5 you can see an unselected checkbox that allows you to convert a label into an anchor. When you tick it, an anchor appears in the Timeline (Figure 9.7) and its presence allows your users to use the Forward and Back buttons in their browser to jump from frame to frame or scene to scene. This is only available to those who are using Flash Player version 6, since its inclusion is new in this edition of Flash.

Frame labels are always included in your final flash movie, so keep them short to cut down on file size. Comments, on the other hand, are stripped out when you publish your movie, so you can make them as long as you like.

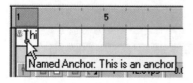

Figure 9.7 An anchor is a special label that allows users to navigate through your Flash movie.

If you are ever in doubt about the use of any Action Script command, click on the little book icon, which you can see on the right hand side of Figure 9.8, and a help frame appears showing the useage, syntax and other comments about the command (Figure 9.9).

Some basic actions

We saw in Figure 9.3 that there are plenty of actions that you can associate with a particular frame. We'll consider just three of them for the moment, though.

The **Stop** and **Play** actions are two of the most fundamental. You add these to any frame to control the playback of the movie at particular points. You might want, for instance, a moving animation to begin and then pause until such time as another action is completed, and then resume once again. You can also override the playback defaults of the finished Shockwave format (.swf) file or projector file – both of which we'll be examining in Chapter 12 – to make them play or pause when first they start up.

When you add either of these actions, there are no additional parameters to enter (Figure 9.8).

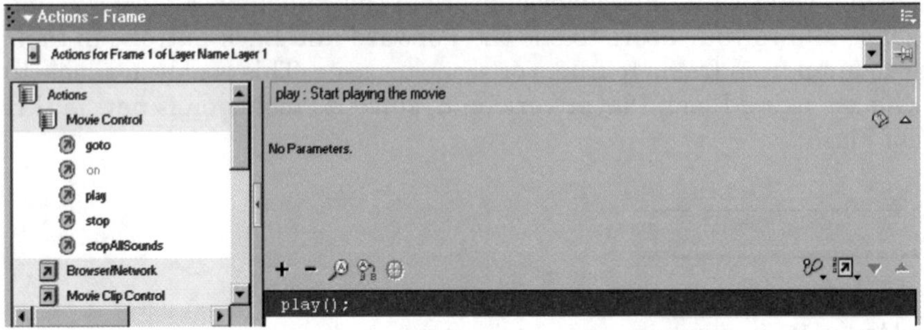

Figure 9.8 Neither Stop nor Play actions need additional parameters.

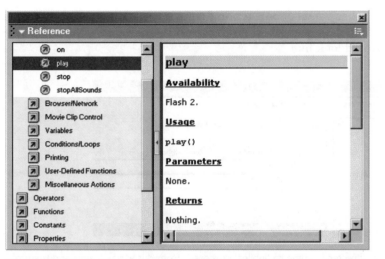

Figure 9.9 The Reference dialog box helps you out with your ActionScript commands.

Unlike the use of Stop and Play, the **Go To** action needs you to enter additional parameters for Flash to know what you want it to do. To make Flash resume playing once it has reached a new location, make sure the radio button that reads **Go to and Play** is checked (Figure 9.10). In the parameters area at the bottom, you can choose which scene to go to (assuming you have more than one, that is!) and which frame to go to (you can choose to go to a frame by its frame number or by a label).

Say, for instance, that we wish our action frame to whisk us away to a frame called *Jubilee* which is in scene 2, then Figure 9.10 shows us what the action parameter box would look like.

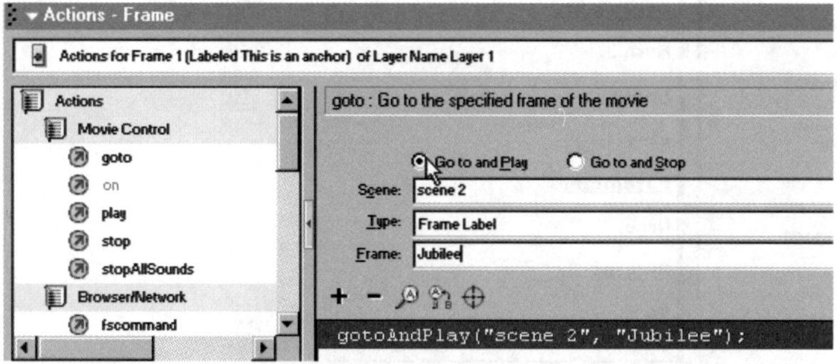

Figure 9.10 Flash is directed to jump to 'Jubilee' in scene 2 from this action frame, and then to start playing straight away.

There is no reason why you could not specify the name of a frame or scene, even if it has not yet been defined – as long as you are organised enough to know in advance what your naming conventions are going to be!

We'll look at some of the expression possibilities later on.

To try out your specified actions, you can use the **Test Movie** or **Test Scene** options in the **Control** menu; if you try simply using Enter in editing mode the actions will, by default, be disabled. This is to stop you being whisked off to destinations unknown when you are trying to work on a specific part of the Timeline. You can, however, switch on the actions by going to your **Control** menu and clicking on **Enable Simple Frame Actions** (Figure 9.11).

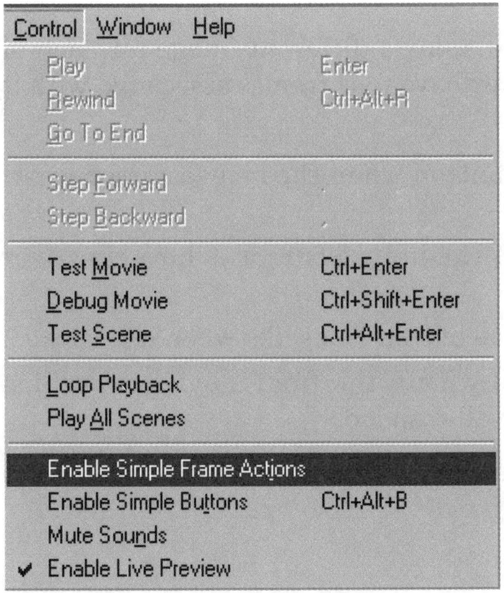

Figure 9.11 Enabling the editor to preview your actions.

BUTTONS

One of the most basic ways in which you can get your audience to participate in the running of your movie is to allow them to interface with the movie by using buttons.

Button states

Buttons are basically symbols that can display a different image for each of their possible states. A button can only ever have four frames associated with it and these are:

1. The **Up** state – which represents the button when the mouse cursor is not over the button.
2. The **Over** state – which occurs when the mouse cursor is hovering over the button.
3. The **Down** state – which shows what the button looks like when it is clicked.
4. The **Hit** state – which you never see within the final movie, but which defines an area over which the button will respond.

It is perfectly acceptable to include movie clips within different button frames to display animated buttons.

Creating a new button

Simple buttons are easily created using basic geometric shapes. If you change characteristics of the shapes within the different button states then it will be easy for your audience to know that your shapes are actually buttons.

Start by creating a new symbol by going to your **Insert** menu and selecting **New Symbol** (Figure 9.12), or by pressing **Ctrl + F8**.

In the Create New Symbol dialog box you can specify a new name for your symbol if you like, but you must select **Button** from the **Behavior** options (Figure 9.13).

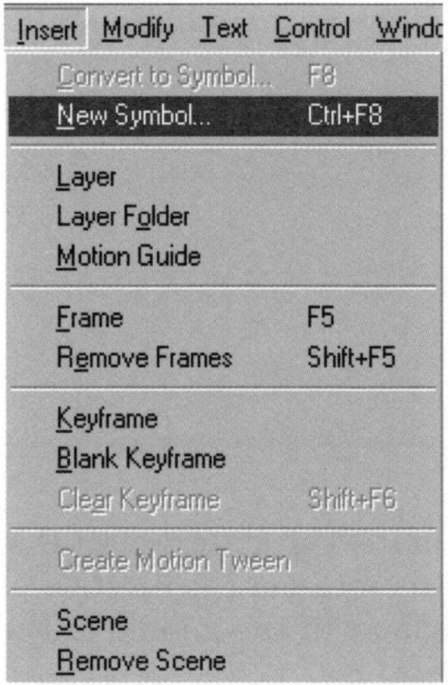

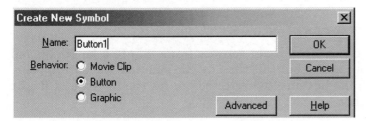

Figure 9.12 Insert a new symbol from the Insert menu.

Figure 9.13 Set the symbol behaviour to Button.

A Timeline for your button is created offering you the four standard states (Figure 9.14).

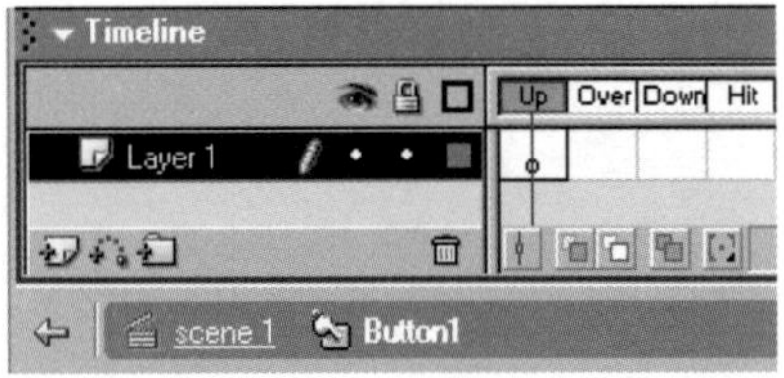

Figure 9.14 Flash creates four states for your new button.

Initially the button has only one empty keyframe in its 'Up' state. Select this frame and then create some graphic on the Stage to represent the up state of the button. It's useful to remember that the crosshair in the middle of the Stage gives you a fixed point of reference to work from.

For this example, we'll choose to place a filled circle as our basic button (Figure 9.15). Once that has been placed we click on frame 2 and make it a keyframe (using right-click). For our 'Over' state we can change its colour fill. (Duplicating the previous keyframe means we can get our alignments sorted out.)

For the 'Down' state we once again convert frame 3 into a keyframe and change the fill colour again; but this time we can simulate the button being 'pushed in' if, with the button state selected, we hit the **Down** and **Right** arrow keys once each.

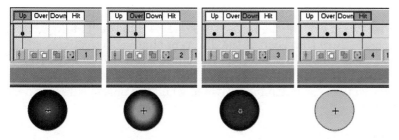

Figure 9.15 The four basic button shapes.

The last 'Hit' state doesn't worry what colours are used. It is only to guide Flash as to which area of the Stage belongs to the button's area of influence. Some people feel comfortable having the entire 'hit' state depicted in some colour such as cyan so that they can immediately recognise it when they see it. For this example we'll once again fill the circle. We can make the hit state slightly bigger than the overall button in order to help the user in determining the button's area.

Once the button has been completed you need to return to movie editing mode (click on 'scene 1' in Figure 9.14). A copy of your button will be placed in the Library and it is from here that you can place an instance of it onto your Stage area.

There is absolutely no reason why you should stick to the same shape for each of your button states. You could have, for instance, a square, a circle and a star for the three 'Up', 'Down' and 'Over' states – just so long as your 'Hit' state is large enough to cover the entire area of the three other states.

Just as when you set frame actions, Flash by default switches off the option of allowing you to view the button states in editing mode. If it didn't, you would find great difficulty in repositioning them or working with them. But to switch off this default you do virtually the same as for frame actions. Go to your **Control** *menu, but this time select* **Enable Simple Buttons**. *However, it is usually best to test your buttons by going to* **Control > Test Scene**.

There is absolutely no reason why the 'Hit' state of a button needs to be in the vicinity of the rest of the button. Nor why there should be only one hot spot. You could have hot spots dotted around the stage if you really wanted to!

An easy way to ensure your 'Hit' state is large enough is to **Edit > Copy** and **Edit > Paste in Place** each of the initial three states into the 'Hit' keyframe. That way you can be sure that each of the different shapes is effectively recognised when you mouse-over the button. You could even use the **Modify > Shape > Expand Fill** by a pixel or two making the 'Hit' area slightly bigger than is necessary so that the button is activated when the mouse cursor is near the actual button.

Interactivity with buttons

Now that we have learned the basics about creating buttons, they can be used for helping the user to interact with your movie. Apart from the normal 'Up', 'Down' and 'Over' states, you can get Flash to react to these same mouse cursor events by completing certain actions. Bring up the **Actions** dialog box and find your way to **Objects > Movie > Button > Events**. As before, we double click on the action to add actions, or click on the '**+**' button to bring up a series of menus to navigate our way to a certain instruction (Figure 9.16).

Let's assign a button to jump to frame 20 of the current scene when it is clicked. First we need to create a blank keyframe in frame 20 and then add anything onto the Stage to identify it. (For instance, type 'frame 20'.) Before we do anything else we need to tell Flash not to move on from frame 1 when we play the movie. To do this, highlight frame 1 and in your **Actions** dialog box go to **Actions > Movie Control** and double-click **Stop**.

In the script pane you will see that the following code has been inserted:

```
Stop();
```

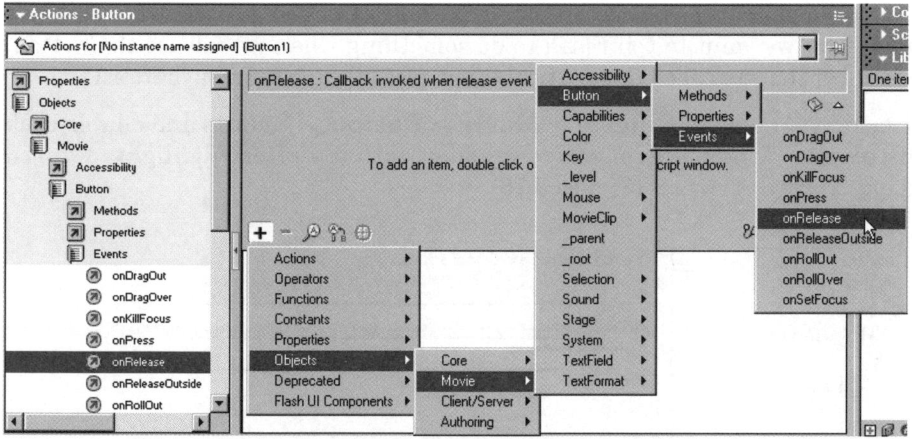

Figure 9.16 Assigning actions to buttons from either the left-hand Actions menu, or by dragging out sub-menus from the '+' button.

Now we'll drag an instance of our button onto the Stage and give it an instance name – let's call it **mybutton1**. Remember, we need to open the **Properties** panel and add the instance name as shown in Figure 9.17.

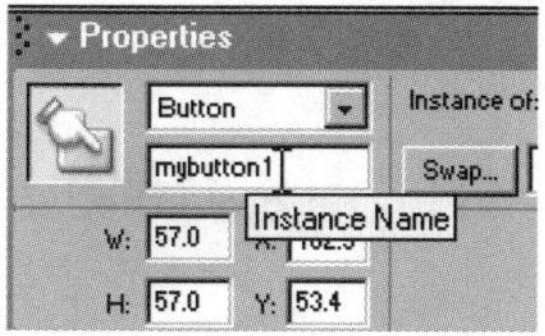

Figure 9.17 Give the button instance a name in the Properties panel.

If we now highlight the frame containing the button we can go back to our **Actions** panel. Now we want to tell Flash to do something when we release the button. Remember that we called this particular instance of the button 'mybutton1'.

Navigate your way to **Objects > Movie > Button > Events** and double-click **onRelease**. A new line of script is added with a section highlighted in red saying <not set yet> (Figure 9.18).

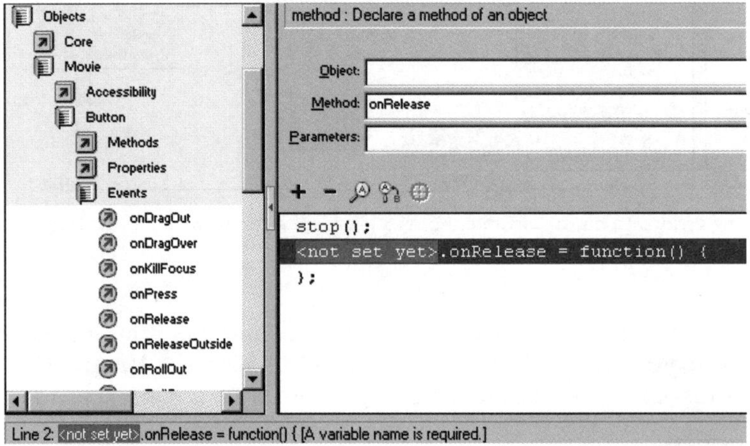

Figure 9.18 ActionScript is waiting for details of the Object to be manipulated.

Well, we've already given a name to our button instance, so in the box labelled **Object** type in mybutton1.

Our ActionScript code should now read:

```
stop()
mybutton1.onRelease = function() {
};
```

Let's consider this for a moment. Those of you familiar with Javascript may well feel at home here.

The semicolon at the end of the script is like a full stop in a sentence. The curly brackets – {} – enclose the instructions for handling an event whilst the straight brackets – ( ) – contain properties relating to the function.

In this case, stop has no properties, so there is nothing added inside the brackets. Similarly, function has no properties at the moment as we still haven't given instructions to Flash as to what to do next. Navigate your way to **Actions > Movie Control**, double-click **goto** and in the dialog box tell it to go to frame 20 and then stop, by clicking on the radio button marked **Go to and Stop** (Figure 9.19).

If you want to add additional events within the 'On (MouseEvent)' and '}' tags, highlight the line above where you want to add an event and then click on the '+' button. The new action will be added immediately below this highlighted line.

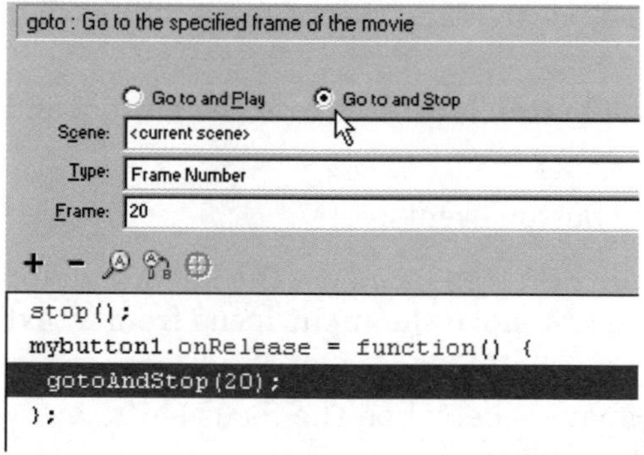

Figure 9.19 We've told Flash to go to Frame 20 when the button is clicked.

All button actions are structured in this way. You will have seen in Figure 9.18 that we could have triggered a button action with other events rather than just the release of the button. For instance:

1. **Press** – occurs when the button is clicked downwards
2. **Release** – occurs when the button is released after it has been clicked down, but only if the cursor is still in the button area. If the button is clicked and then the mouse dragged off the button before being let go, then the action will not happen.
3. **Release Outside** – is the opposite of Release, in that the mouse must be outside the button's area before being released after clicking, otherwise the action will not happen.
4. **Roll Over** – will occur any time that the mouse invades the button's hit area
5. **Roll Out** – occurs whenever the mouse rolls out of the button's active area
6. **Drag Over** – works when the user holds down the mouse within the button area, rolls the cursor outside of the active area and then returns within that area once more.
7. **Drag Out** – happens when the mouse button is pressed over the button, and the pointer is then moved out of the active area

In addition, Flash MX includes two new button events:

8. **Set Focus** is invoked when a button receives focus via the keyboard, for instance when the Tab key is pressed to move the input focus from a text field to the button.
9. **Kill Focus** is the opposite of the above – i.e. when the focus shifts away from the button to another object on the Stage.

So, buttons can get your movie to react in different ways, depending on whether, for instance, you click the button or move the cursor over the button.

When you assign actions from the action list there is no reason why you cannot stack them so that, for instance, you can issue one set of commands dependent on **Roll Over** and another one on **Roll Out** and a third on **Release** (Figure 9.20).

```
stop();
mybutton1.onRelease = function() {
  gotoAndStop(20);
};
mybutton1.onRollOver = function() {
  gotoAndPlay(30);
};
mybutton1.onRollOut = function() {
  gotoAndPlay(40);
};
```

Figure 9.20 Multiple-choice actions.

So far we've only scratched the surface of Flash interactivity. But before we move on to more advanced scripting techniques in Chapter 11, we need to learn a little about the use of sound in Flash.

Buttons don't actually have to have any graphics on them at all. Instead you could use what are referred to as 'Invisible Buttons'. As long as the hit frame has content, then you can ask your users to click anywhere within an area of the screen to launch the next action. This might be useful if, for instance, you wanted to pause an interactive presentation and let your users resume play simply by clicking anywhere.

Sound 10

How Flash handles sounds

Importing sounds

Adding sounds to frames

Adding sounds to buttons

Sync settings

Streaming sounds

Making simple edits to your sound files

Just as the arrival of pictures on Websites revolutionised the entire way in which the World Wide Web was used, and was the main reason that its use grew in such a spectacular fashion, so too is the use of sound on Websites becoming all pervasive across the Internet.

How Flash handles sounds

Flash can handle sounds that have been recorded in WAV and MP3 formats. MP3 files are, by definition, smaller than WAV files because of their in-built compression, and if you can you should import these in preference to WAV, although Flash MX does compress sounds on export. Additionally, if you have QuickTime version 4 on your computer, you can import Sun AU, AIFF and QuickTime sound files.

Sounds can be used either as one-off events (such as a click sound when a button is pressed) or as a streaming sound that, for instance, delivers background music as your movie progresses. These two types of sound are handled differently by Flash and it is important to understand where the main differences lie:

- An **event** sound has to download completely before it can play. It will then keep on playing until instructed to stop.
- A **streaming** sound starts to play as soon as enough information has been downloaded for the first few frames. Thereafter the sound is synchronised to the Timeline as Flash forces the frames to keep in pace with the sound.

Importing sounds

You import sounds in exactly the same way you would import bitmaps and other artwork. From the **File** menu choose **Import** or **Import to Library** and select the file type to read **WAV**, **MP3** or **All Sound Formats** before selecting your particular sound (Figure 10.1).

*You can import as many sound files as you like in one go by holding down the **Ctrl** key as you select the different files.*

Look in:	SOUNDS		
ABOARD.WAV	CUCKOO01.WAV	HORSE1.WAV	RATTLER.W,
AWARGLIS.WAV	DIESEL.WAV	HSTINGER.WAV	ROOSTER.W
AZIPGLIS.WAV	DOGBARK.WAV	HUH.WAV	RSTAB1.WA\
BCRASH.WAV	DONKEY.WAV	KAZOO.WAV	SCREAM.WA
BESSIE.WAV	FERSURE.WAV	LASER2.WAV	SEALION.WA
BIGHORN.WAV	GAMESHOW.WAV	LEAR.WAV	SHEEP1.WA\
BIGSKID.WAV	GARGLE.WAV	MUSFALL.WAV	SNARE.WAV
CASH2.WAV	HEADSHAK.WAV	OHNO.WAV	SNEEZE.WA'
CHICK.WAV	HELP.WAV	ONERING.WAV	SOSURE.WA
COMICD.WAV	HICCUP.WAV	OUCH.WAV	TAXIF.WAV
CREAROAR.WAV	HORRORBL.WAV	OWL.WAV	TRASH.WAV

File name:	CHICK.WAV	Open
Files of type:	All Sound Formats	Cancel

Figure 10.1 Importing sound files.

Flash imports the files directly into its Library (regardless of which import option you just chose) for you to use as required. Remember, you can inspect the Library contents by pressing **F11** if it is not already docked to your panel collection and in the preview window you will see the waveform for each selected sound file. Clicking on the play button allows you to hear what the file sounds like (Figure 10.2).

You can enlarge the height of individual layers and by doing so it is possible to see more of the waveform of the sounds for better placing graphics and action files. To enlarge a layer within your Timeline select **Modify > Layer** *and set the layer height to* **100%** *(normal),* **200%** *or* **300%***.*

Figure 10.2 You can 'preview' your sound files directly in the Library window.

Although there is nothing to stop you adding sounds to graphics layers, you will find it easier to allocate separate layers to individual sounds and to keep these layers together so that you can easily find particular sounds when it's time to update or edit them. It's quite a good idea to group them all in one sounds folder (Figure 10.3).

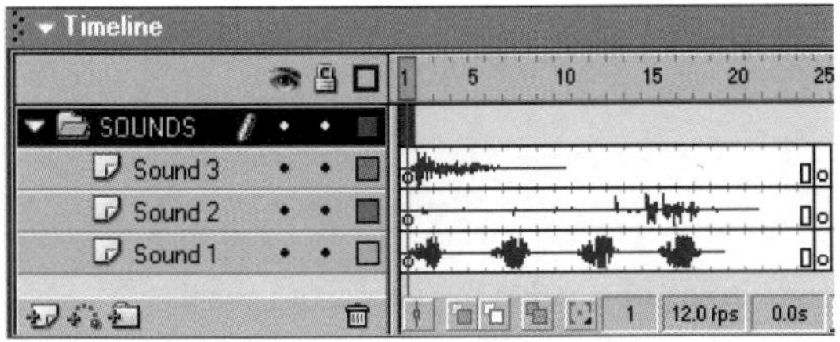

Figure 10.3 Add sound layers within a folder for easy identification.

Adding sound to frames

You can assign any sound that is currently in your movie's library by dragging it to the Stage once you have selected, or created, a keyframe. It obviously doesn't matter where you drop the sound file on the Stage since the sound is 'invisible'; but as you drop the file onto the Stage Flash will attach that sound file to the particular keyframe you have selected.

Apart from adding a sound instance by dragging it from the Movie's library, you can also add it via the **Sound** dialog box found within the **Properties** panel. You can inspect the **Sound** drop-down menu to select the sound from the movie's library (Figure 10.4).

We'll return to the other options in this dialog box in a short while.

Figure 10.4 Selecting a sound from the Sound dialog box within the Properties panel.

Adding sounds to buttons

It can be very useful for your viewers to have sounds allocated to your buttons. Apart from adding a touch of reality, they can also help to highlight 'hot spots' when the cursor is moved over them.

Pull a button onto your Stage (we'll use the 'push button – orange' from the Buttons library for this example) and with your button visible, right-click on it and choose **Edit** to open it up in symbol-editing mode. Add a new layer at the top of the button's Timeline and label it *Sounds*. We now want to assign two sounds to the button – one when the user's cursor hovers over it and another when the button is actually clicked.

First, then, you need to **Insert > Blank Keyframes** into both the **Over** and **Down** states on this sounds layer. Then you assign sounds to each of these two keyframes in the way we have just described. You should see a Timeline similar to that shown in Figure 10.5.

Once you are happy with the placing of the sounds, you can return to movie-editing mode by clicking on the **Scene 1** button shown at the left of Figure 10.5. Remember that you can only 'preview' the sounds by first selecting **Control > Enable Simple Buttons**.

There is no reason why you cannot allocate sounds to the 'Up' and 'Hit' states of the button. In these cases, you would hear the particular sounds when you either rolled the cursor out of the button's area, or when you released the button within the active hit area respectively.

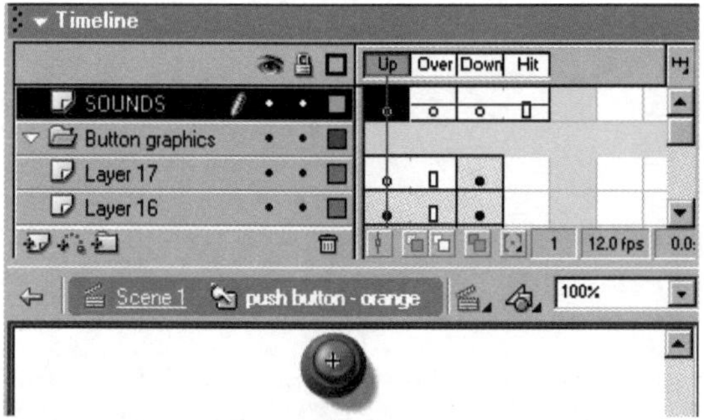

Figure 10.5 Adding sounds to a button.

Sync settings

We saw in Figure 10.4 that there were other drop-down menus, which were pertinent to the way that sounds played along the Timeline. If we begin by looking at the **Sync** drop-down menu, we can see there are four options (Figure 10.6):

1. event;
2. start;
3. stop;
4. stream.

By default, Flash sets a sound to play as an *Event*. This means that the beginning of the sound is set to a particular keyframe, regardless of what is happening around it in the rest of the movie.

Figure 10.6 Choosing a Sync Setting.

This can impact your movie in two dramatic ways. For instance, as all the information to play an *Event* sound is contained within a specific keyframe, Flash will pause to download all the sound information from that particular frame and only then continue with the rest of the movie once it has done. This means that you should only use short sounds as *Event* sounds, otherwise your movie could become jerky as it stops and starts waiting for long sounds to download.

Another aspect of the *Event* choice is that, were a sound to be longer than the overall length of the section of your movie in which it is contained, then it will keep on playing even after that section has come to an end. The way to stop this happening is to insert a Stop command ....

Choose where you want your particular sound to stop and insert a blank keyframe. Although this has the effect of cutting off your view of the waveform in the Timeline, the sound will continue to play. However, if you now go to the sound panel dialog box for this blank keyframe, you can specify in the **Sync** menu to stop the sound and also specify the name of the particular sound you want stopped.

To let you know a Stop command has been issued, Flash places a small square in the Timeline where the sound ends (Figure 10.7)

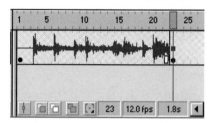

Figure 10.7 A Stop Command is shown by the little black square.

Adding two sounds simultaneously

Flash can play as many sounds simultaneously as you like. However, only one sound can be assigned to each keyframe, so this means that if you want two sounds to start at the same frame, then each must be assigned to a separate layer. (Remember, though, that the more sounds Flash has to download, the longer will be the pause at this particular frame.)

Alternatively, if you want one sound to start after another, but for both sounds to be playing simultaneously, it is quite in order for the two sounds to be placed on the same layer, as long as they are not instructed to start in the same frame.

Start sounds

At first encounter, it appears that *Start* sounds has an almost identical behaviour pattern to *Event* sounds. After all, the sound is set in train when a specific keyframe is encountered.

We referred just now to the scene looping. And just as a scene or movie can loop (when frame actions are set this way), so too can a sound be made to loop a specific number of times. If you look at Figure 10.6 you will see there is a dialog box in which you can specify the number of times a sound should loop.

The important difference, however, is that with a *Start* sound instruction, only one instance of this sound can play at any one time, whereas with an *Event* sound, you can have multiple instances of the same sound playing simultaneously.

This means that if, for instance, a movie is set to loop and the sound that kicks off in the first loop playback is still playing when this frame repeats, then:

- if the sound is an *Event* sound you will hear two instances of the sound playing simultaneously (but not necessarily in sync);
- if the sound is a *Start* sound, only the first instance will play, and there will be no repeat until such time as the first instance of the sound has stopped and the scene has looped again to hit the keyframe containing the sound.

Streaming sounds

Unlike Event sounds that must be completely downloaded before they can play, *Streaming Sounds* start playing once only a fraction of the information has downloaded. By setting the **Sync** to **Stream**, Flash synchronises it with specific frames of your movie and plays the sound until either a new keyframe is encountered, or a Stop command is issued.

In Streaming Audio, Flash subdivides the sound into clips whose length is proportional to the overall frame rate. So, if the frame rate is set to the default of 12 frames per second, each clip of sound is created to last 1/12th of a second. Each of these subclips is timed to start with each new frame encountered, but if the sound is too fast for the images, Flash sacrifices some of the frames to keep up with the sounds. This could have the effect of making the movie look jerky, but that is simply one of the downsides to streaming audio against a fixed frame rate.

With streaming sounds, you can hear how the sound interacts with the different frames by 'scrubbing' along the Timeline. Drag the playhead across the Timeline and see how the sound peaks coincide with different aspects of the graphic frame contents (Figure 10.8).

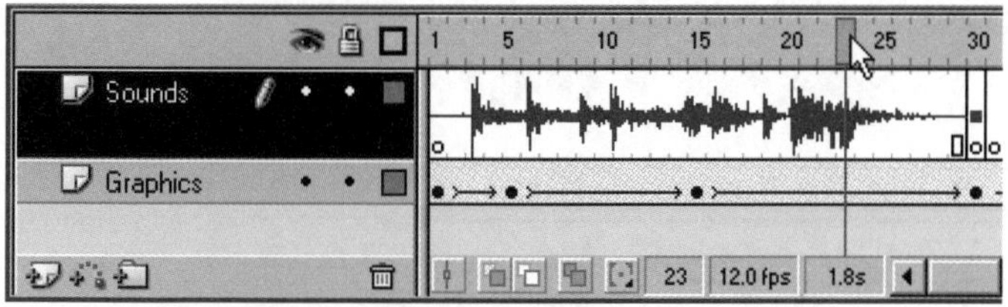

Figure 10.8 'Scrubbing' along the Timeline.

If the synchronisation is not to your liking, you can add or delete frames to get the timing better. This can be made simpler if you switch between different views in your **Edit Envelope** dialog box, which can be accessed by clicking on the **Edit** button in the sound panel. You can view the sound sequence in either frame view or time view by clicking on one of the right hand icons at the bottom of the edit envelope (Figure 10.9) and thereby deduce exactly how many frames you need to add or delete to make your sound file fit your frames sequence.

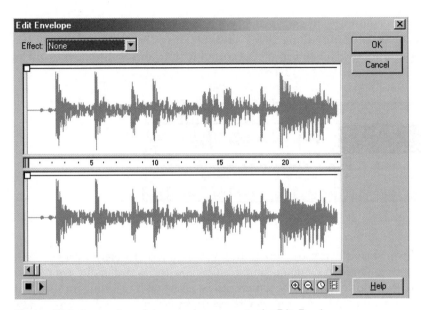

Figure 10.9 Frame view of the sound sequence in the Edit Envelope.

Making simple edits to your sound files

To a limited degree, Flash allows you to make superficial edits to your sound files. You can alter:

- the start and end points of the sound;
- its volume;
- the relationship between the left and right stereo channels.

(However, for any serious editing it is probably better to edit the sound files in programs specific to the task.)

To change the volume of sound files with Flash, you begin by opening up the **Edit Envelope** as we did just a moment ago.

The **Effect** tab is where you can choose one of the following:

- none;
- left Channel;
- right Channel;
- fade Left to Right;
- fade Right to Left;
- fade In;
- fade Out;
- custom.

As you can see in Figure 10.10, the volume levels of both right and left channels can be set by dragging the envelope handles up or down. Choose one of the cross fade or fade in/out options, and the volume levels are set automatically.

You can add more handles by clicking on the waveform – to a maximum of eight per channel – and each can then be dragged up or down, left or right, to change the volume levels along the playback line of the sound file (Figure 10.11).

As we have already mentioned, Flash's sound editing is pretty basic, but it does allow for some simple effects. If you are likely to want to cut back the overall length of many of your sound files it may still be worth doing so in an external sound-editing program since, although Flash can be set to ignore the start and end points of the sound, the overall file is still contained in the final Flash movie. This just takes up unnecessary space, making your final movie bigger than it needs to be.

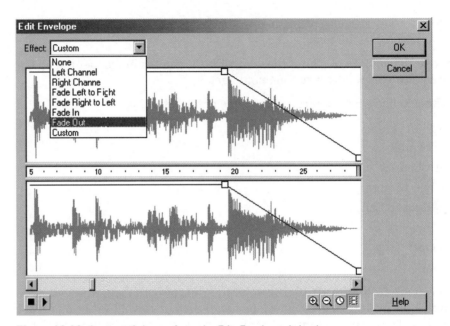

Figure 10.10 Setting a fade-out from the Edit Envelope dialog box.

To remove unwanted envelope handles you simply drag them from the window. To hear the resulting sound, click on the play icon shown in the bottom left-hand corner of Figure 10.11.

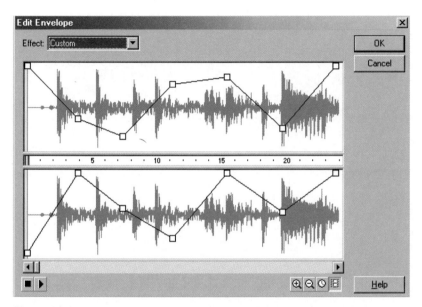

Figure 10.11 A sound file can contain up to eight handles – for each channel.

More complex interactivity and components

Creating a hyperlink

Window states

E-mailing from within a Flash movie

Components

Passing variables

Expert Mode

We've seen how Flash allows you to interact with your movies in a number of ways – not least through the use of actions sparked off by clicking buttons or the choice of specific items on menus. With the arrival of version 4, Macromedia introduced complex interactivity into Flash for the first time; it introduced variables and expressions allowing the site designer to use formulaic interactivity that would test for certain conditions and carry out an action specific to the outcome of a particular test.

With Flash 5 Macromedia made another major leap forward in introducing a scripting language based on JavaScript, which it calls *ActionScript*. Flash MX has taken ActionScript a long way forward and, once you have understood the basics of how it all works, even those with no programming experience can get some quite complex interactivity embedded into their Flash movies.

Using expressions and variables in Flash takes a little while to grasp. Many people find it much more difficult to come to grips with than other aspects of the design of a Flash production. However, we would strongly recommend working through the following pages, trying out the expressions for yourself and learning by experimentation. That way you should find that what appears daunting at first opens out a whole new vista for your site development and brings Flash into a realm of its own.

There are books available devoted solely to ActionScript that are many times larger than this; so it would not be possible in a book this size to go into too much detail about everything on offer. However, by working through this chapter you will get a good idea of the kind of things that ActionScript can offer you and it should make experimentation with the remaining features that much simpler to grasp.

Creating a hyperlink

Flash is not just a program for creating special effects and animations. It is also used extensively for navigation and other interactive purposes. Just as hyperlinks are the basis for HTML and navigating around the World Wide Web, so too can you use hyperlinks within the Flash authoring environment.

Creating a hyperlink in Flash is quite straightforward, but it does require a modicum of understanding how ActionScript works. By going through the following example we'll pick up some pointers on the way.

We'll begin by creating a new document by going to **File > New**. From the **Tools** panel, click the **Oval** tool and draw a circle on the stage. Once the circle has been drawn, select it with your mouse pointer and press **F8** or go to **Insert > Convert to Symbol**. The Convert to Symbol dialog box appears (Figure 11.1).

Figure 11.1 Turn your circle into a button when you convert it to a symbol.

URL is short for Uniform Resource Locator, which, in Internet terms, is a way of specifying a Website address. An absolute URL gives information about the server on which the Website is located, the path to the Website itself and the name of the file being called. A relative URL, on the other hand, describes the address of the file relative to the current page being displayed. When testing your movies on your computer, relative URLs allow you to specify files on your computer in relation to others rather than making you get onto the Internet to find an absolute address.

In the **Name** field, give this circle a name (we'll call it *'Hyperlink'*) and in the **Behavior** section, select the **Button** option. Press **OK** to close the dialog box. The circle now acts as a button, even though there is only one 'state' – i.e. nothing changes when you hover over it or click on it. Right click on the circle and select **Actions**. The Actions panel will expand for you to input actions.

Click on the + icon and navigate your way to **Actions > Browser/ Network > getURL**. You will see URL, Window, and Variables fields displayed (Figure 11.2).

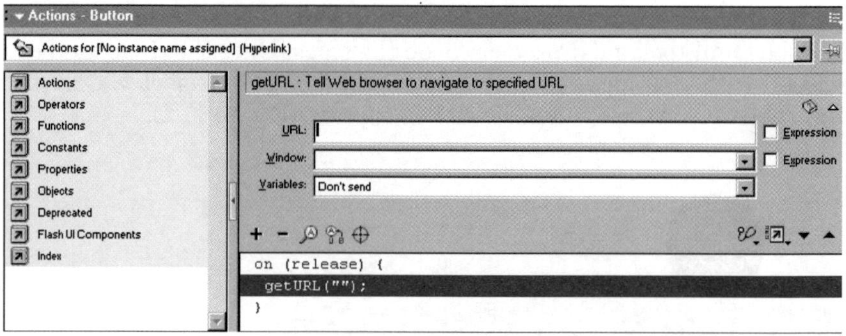

Figure 11.2 The Actions panel awaits your input.

In the **URL** field enter a Web address. As an example, we'll enter **'http://www.topspin-group.com'**. Click the **Window** field/drop-down menu and select **_blank**. Notice how, as you fill in the appropriate fields, the ActionScript is filled out with your inputted text (Figure 11.3).

```
getURL : Tell Web browser to navigate to specified URL

URL:      http://www.topspin-group.com          □ Expression
Window:   _blank                            ▼    □ Expression
Variables: Don't send                        ▼

+  -  ⌕ ⚭ ⊕                          ∞, ⬈, ▼ ▲

on (release) {
    getURL ("http://www.topspin-group.com", "_blank");
}
```

Figure 11.3 ActionScript completes automatically as you enter information into the text fields.

In Figure 11.3, we have entered an absolute URL address. Obviously, this is a text string, so we don't click on the **Expression** box. If we had, Flash would have come up with a warning (Figure 11.4) in glorious Technicolor that is impossible to miss!

Finally you can determine whether you want Flash to **GET** or **POST** variables (or not to pass any at all) to your URL address. This is useful if you need to send variables to a CGI script, which generates a .swf file as its CGI output. (We'll get more familiar with Shockwave – .swf – file formats in the next chapter.) If you aren't familiar with CGI commands you are probably best leaving this option set to **Don't send**.

Now if you go to **Control > Test Movie** two things will happen. When you bring the mouse cursor over your circle, the cursor will turn into a hand to show you are over a hyperlink, and (if you are on-line) clicking on the circle will bring up a new browser window with your chosen Website.

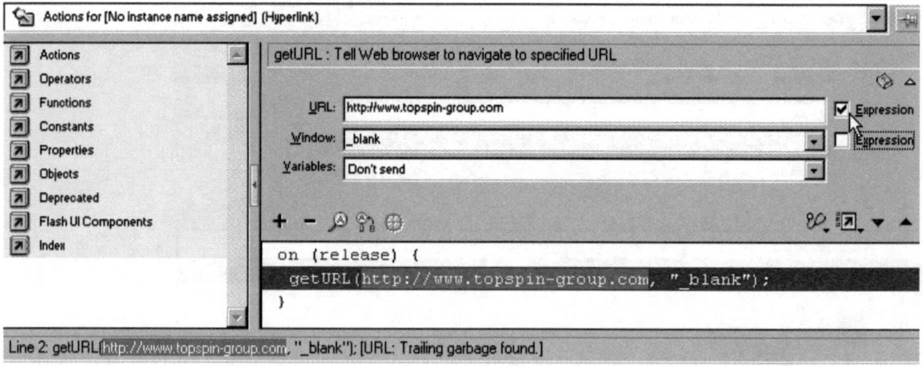

Figure 11.4 Flash tells us, in the nicest possible way, that we've written 'garbage'!

Window states

Sometimes you may not want every link to open in a new window. Maybe you want the link to open in the current window. That is where the **Window** field of the button Actions plays a large role.

1. **_blank** forces the new URL to be loaded into a new window.

2. **_self** specifies the current frame in the current window.

3. **_parent** loads the URL into the current frame's parent.

4. **_top** ensures the URL is loaded into the top level frame within the current window.

E-mailing from within a Flash movie

A variation on getting Flash to load a Web page is to get it to send an e-mail for you. Both use the **getURL** command.

We'll take a look at three, very basic ways, of sending e-mail from Flash using a standard HTML '*mailto*' routine. Each of the methods makes use of your visitors' own e-mail program to send the message. As such, there is no CGI or ASP scripting to worry about.

The first method uses a standard Flash button to launch the visitor's e-mail program. Open up a new movie and add some suitable text asking the visitor to click on a button in order to send an e-mail. (Remember to use *static* text in your text box.)

From the **Common Libraries** panel, select **Buttons**, choose a suitable button from the menu and drag it onto the Stage (Figure 11.5).

Figure 11.5 Drag a button onto your Stage area.

*In this book we'll mainly be sticking with **Normal** mode. If, however, you are happy with getting your hands dirty in lines of computer code, then maybe you'll be comfortable working in **Expert Mode**. This is what separates the men from the boys. In Expert Mode:*

- *no parameter fields appear. You have to hard code the expressions yourself;*
- *the Up and Down arrows are switched off;*
- *in the button panel, only the Add (+) button works. You have to manually delete anything you don't want.*

With your button highlighted, open the **Actions** Panel and click on the **Options** icon to ensure that **Normal Mode** is selected (Figure 11.6).

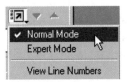

Figure 11.6 Selecting Normal mode from the Options icon.

Go to your Actions panel and navigate to **Actions > Movie Control** and double-click **on**. A choice of **Events** appears with **Release** already pre-selected (Figure 11.7). You will see the `on (release) { }` command appear on line 1 in the code window on the right-hand side.

This is another way of coding a button action. In Chapter 9 we used the **Objects > Movie > Button > Events** path to reach **onRelease**; as you can see, this is a much faster route to the same piece of code.

Whichever route you take to this point, you now have to tell Flash what you want the button to do. Navigate to **Actions > Browser/Network** and double-click on **getURL**. In the **URL** field enter 'mailto:you@youraddress.com', substituting your own e-mail address for the 'you@youraddress.com' bit, of course (Figure 11.8).

Actions
Movie Control
goto
on
play
stop
stopAllSounds
Browser/Network
Movie Clip Control
Variables
Conditions/Loops
Printing
on : Performs actions when a particular mouse event o
Event:
Press
Release
Release Outside
Key Press:
Roll Over
Roll Out
Drag Over
Drag Out
on (release) {
}

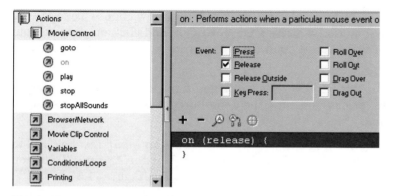

Figure 11.7 Choose which button action you want from the Event menu.

getURL : Tell Web browser to navigate to specified URL
URL:
mailto:brian@topspin-group.com
Expression
Window:
Expression
Variables:
Don't send
on (release) {
getURL("mailto:brian@topspin-group.com");
}

Figure 11.8 Add a `mailto:` command to convert the URL into an e-mail address.

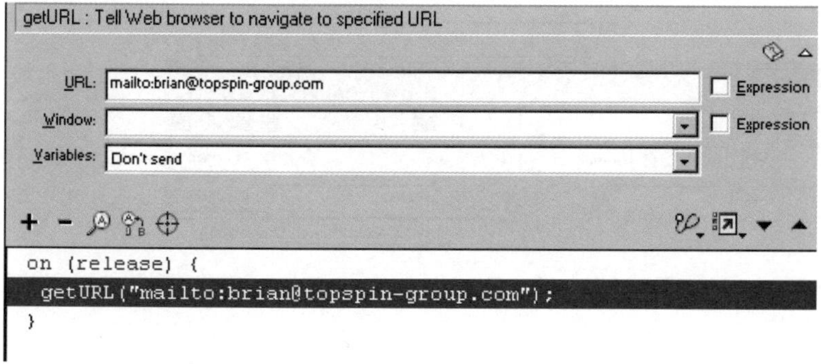

So why would anyone want to switch to Expert Mode? Well, it lets advanced users edit their scripts in an ordinary text editor just as they would JavaScript or VBScript. Unless you're proficient and confident in your programming abilities, you're probably best sticking with Normal mode, although we'll have a go at Expert Mode later in this chapter.

The Show Border Around Text command is important for your users to know where to input their text. If you leave it out, they will have to guess where the input field is.

A Variable is an identifier for holding data. They can be changed and updated and the values they store can be retrieved for use in other parts of the program. In the expression 'x = 10', x is a variable which has the value 10.

Once again, all the code is filled in for you. If you now choose **Test Movie** from the **Control** menu (or press **Ctrl + Enter**) and click on your button, your e-mail program should open, ready for your visitors to compose and send a message.

So far, so good. In the next exercise we're going to gather some information from our visitors, prior to opening the e-mail program, and we'll take a first look at *components*.

Start once again by opening a new movie and create an *Input Text* box. Fill in the variable box as '*recipient*'. Click on the **Show Border Around Text** icon and use a *Static Text* box to give your input box a name (Figure 11.9).

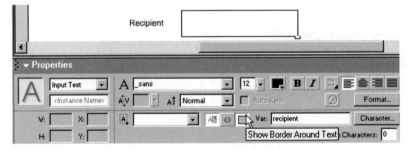

Figure 11.9 Creating an Input Text box with set variable and borders.

Now create another *Input Text* box and name its variable '*subject*'. Give it a static text name as before. Finally add a *Multiline Input Text* box, name its variable '*body*' and give it a static text name (Figure 11.10).

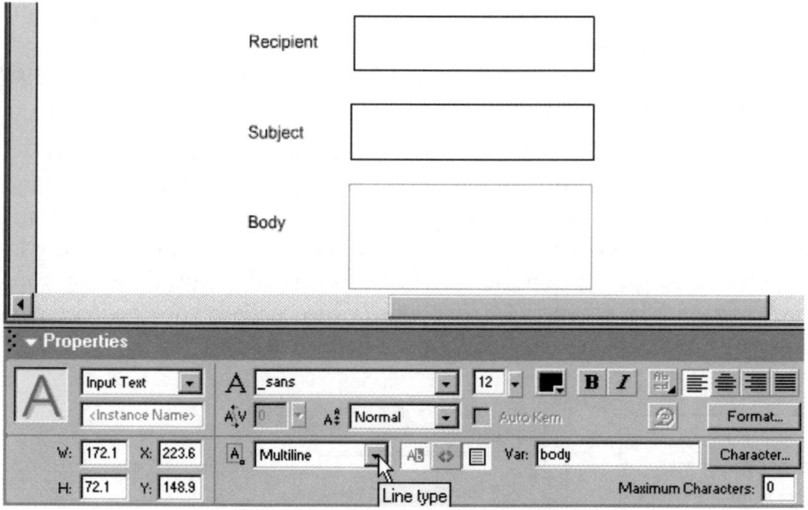

Figure 11.10 Our stage should now contain three text boxes with static text tables.

Components

We're now going to use one of Flash's library of **components**. These are complex movie clips which, because they are used so often, can be stored in their own library and used by all your different Flash movies. Earlier editions of Flash used what were known as *Smart Clips*, but in this version of Flash, Macromedia has added a library of ActionScripted components ready for you to use.

*Notice that you can drag the scrollbar to another part of the Stage if you want to. The text box and scrollbar do not have to be docked together in your final movie. If you want to have a horizontal scrollbar instead of a vertical one, highlight the scrollbar itself and in the **Properties** panel change the **Horizontal** control from False to **True**.*

Each of these components is a Flash movie extension in its own right that you can use and customise to your own specifications. (If you look at the Websites recommended at the end of this book, some of them contain extra components that you can download and add to your library.)

Let's see how they work. We're going to add a scrollbar to the multiline box we just created. Open the **Components** panel on the right-hand side of the Stage area (or press **Ctrl + F7** if it is not already open) and drag the 'ScrollBar' component into the body text box (Figure 11.11). You will see a scrollbar appear in the text box. All the scripting to make it work has already been done for you, and as you will see shortly, when the text needs to be scrolled, your visitors will be able to do so quite normally without any further work from you!

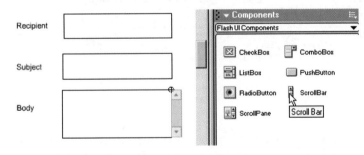

Figure 11.11 Adding a scrollbar is simply a matter of a drag-and-drop.

We want to have a button for our visitors to press, so from the **Window** menu select **Common Libraries > Buttons** and drag a suitable button onto the Stage. With the button selected (it will be shown as being surrounded by a blue square) open the **Actions** window in **Normal** mode. Open the **Movie Control** menu, double-click on **on** and tick the **Release** checkbox.

Now, with the button still selected, open the **Browser > Network** menu and double click on **getURL**. We want to enter an expression now, rather than rely on it all to be pre-coded, so ensure the **Expression** checkbox next to the URL field is ticked. In the **URL** field type the following (Figure 11.12):

```
"mailto:" +recipient+ "?subject=" +subject+ "&body=" +body
```

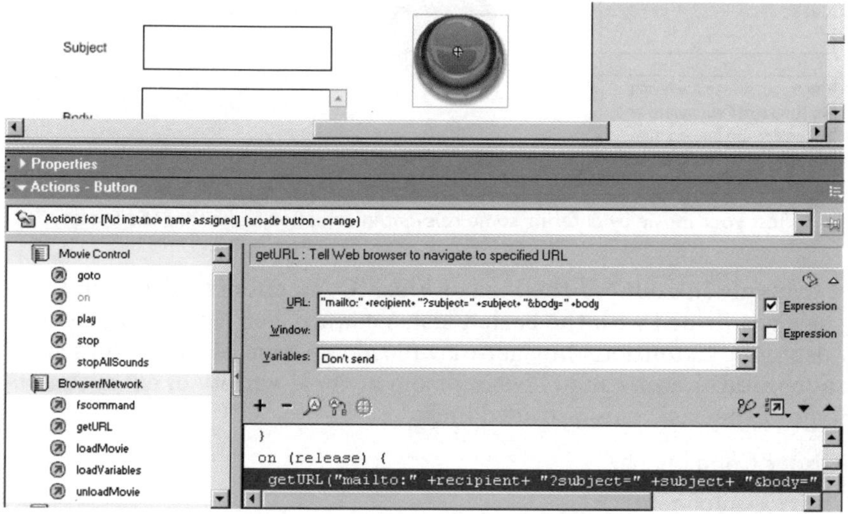

An **Expression** is a type of formula made up of a mathematical combination of **variables**. Variables, which can be added or amended by the viewer of the movie, are called **concrete variables**. Variables that exist only in the inner workings of Flash, but over which the viewer has no control, are called **abstract variables**.

Figure 11.12 Ensure the Expression box is ticked if you intend to enter an expression.

This has the effect of passing the contents of the input text box variables (recipient, subject and body) to your e-mail program once the button is released. Leave the other fields as they are.

Your form should now resemble Figure 11.13. Go to **Control > Test Movie** to test that it all works.

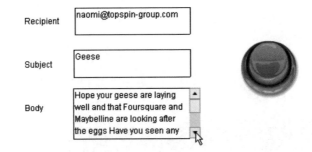

Figure 11.13 Test your movie by entering some relevant information and hitting the button.

This last example introduced the idea of Flash Components. Although there are only seven provided with the basic Flash software, you can add a whole lot more by using the Extension Manager (downloadable from Macromedia's site – **www.macromedia.com**) and choosing from a whole variety of extra components. Some of the basic ones provided include:

- **LineChart** Component;
- **BarChart** Component;
- **PieChart** Component;

- **Calendar** Component for creating a graphical display of a month;
- **DraggablePane** Component for enclosing content in a movable, scrollable pane;
- **IconButton** Component for creating a button with a custom icon and custom look;
- **MessageBox** Component for creating dialog boxes;
- **ProgressBar** Component for creating preloading progress sequences;
- **SplitView** Component for the layout of complex data or image views;
- **Ticker** Component for scrolling data repeatedly through its window;
- **Tree** Component for creating a classic tree view of related data elements.

For our next example we're going to explore the *getURL* command a bit further and create a cut-down version of the previous form in which we will pre-define the recipient and subject, leaving just the body of the form for the visitor to fill in.

Create a new movie in the normal way and use the static text function to insert a heading for the form. Now create a *Multiline Input Text* box and name the variable *'body'*. Add a scrollbar as we did in the previous example.

Next we'll need a button, so go to the **Common Libraries > Buttons** panel and drag a suitable button onto the Stage. (Don't be tempted to use the *push button* from the components panel as it doesn't work with the techniques outlined in this example.)

With the button selected (surrounded by a blue square) open the **Actions** window in **Normal** mode, then go to the **Movie Control** menu, double-click on **on** and tick the **Release** checkbox. With the button still selected, open the

Browser/Network menu and double-click on **getURL** Make sure that the **Expression** checkbox next to the URL field is ticked and in this field type the following (Figure 11.14):

```
"mailto:you@youraddress.com?subject=Feedback" + "&body=" +body
```

When you run the movie and click on the button, the contents of the variable *body* will be passed to the e-mail program ready for mailing to the address you have defined (you@youraddress.com). Test out your movie in the normal way by going to **Control > Test Movie**.

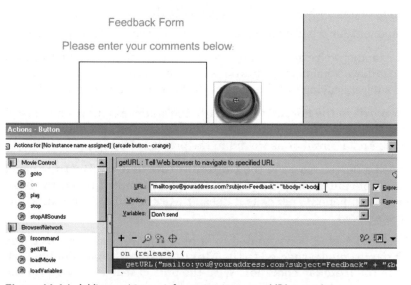

Figure 11.14 Adding `mailto:` information into your URL input box.

Passing variables

One of the most important uses for variables is in their ability to pass information from one part of the program to another. In this example, we'll create a form into which a visitor can enter their name. Next we'll use one of the buttons from the *Common Libraries* panel as a *Submit* button that passes the *name* variable to another frame for processing. Finally, we'll create a piece of ActionScript that creates a greeting depending on the time of day. Flash will then display a Good Morning / Afternoon / Evening greeting along with the visitor's name which is passed across to it via the name variable.

Start by creating a new movie and give it a background colour (solely in this example so that we can see what is going on). Go to the Timeline and double-lick where it says Layer 1 and rename the layer *'objects'*. Click on the **Insert Layer** icon to create a new layer and rename it *'scripts'* (Figure 11.15).

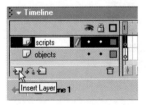

Figure 11.15 Here we've renamed two layers to help us track what we are doing.

Now click on the **objects** layer to select it and, with the text tool selected, click on the Stage and drag a large text box. In the **Properties Inspector** panel, select **Static Text** and choose a suitable font. Enter some text such as *'Enter your name'*.

Making sure that the **objects** layer is still selected, drag another text box onto the Stage and from the **Properties Inspector** panel select **Input Text**. (You will see that, as expected, the small square drag handle now moves to the bottom of the text box.) Click on the **Show Border Around Text** icon, and in the **Var** field type '*name*'. As before, this will attach a variable called *name* to the text box (Figure 11.16).

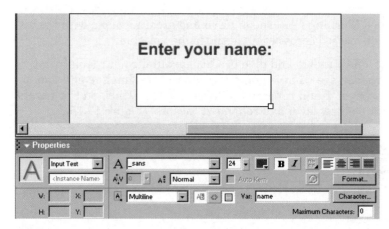

Figure 11.16 Give your variable field a label – in this case 'name'.

With the objects layer still selected, drag a suitable button from the **Common Libraries > Buttons** area onto the Stage (Figure 11.17).

Figure 11.17 Add a button to the Stage.

Now you need to right-click on frame 2 in the objects layer and **Insert > Blank Keyframe**. Use the **Text** tool to drag a new text box on the Stage, and in the **Properties** panel for the text box, select **Dynamic Text** and choose your font properties. Unclick the **Show Border Around Text** icon if it is selected, as in this example we don't want a border showing in our final movie. In the **Var** field, enter '*hello*'.

Repeat the process to create a second text box beneath the first. Once again select **Dynamic Text** in the properties panel and deselect the **Show Border Around Text** icon if it is selected. Name the variable '*guest*' (Figure 11.18).

Now go back to the Timeline, select the **scripts** layer and right-click in frame 2 of that layer. Select **Insert > Keyframe** from the menu. Your Timeline should resemble Figure 11.19.

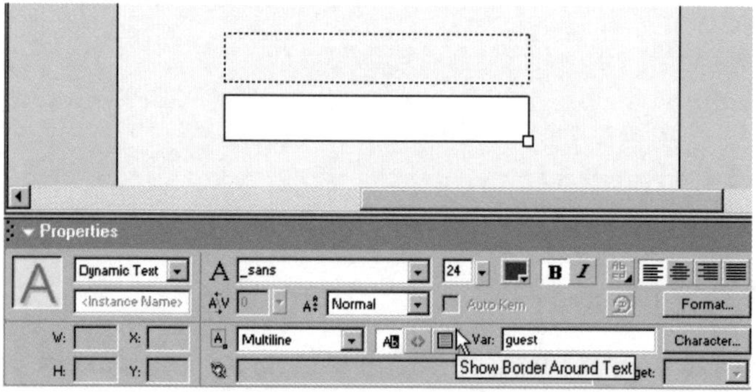

Figure 11.18 Here we have two dynamic boxes with no borders showing.

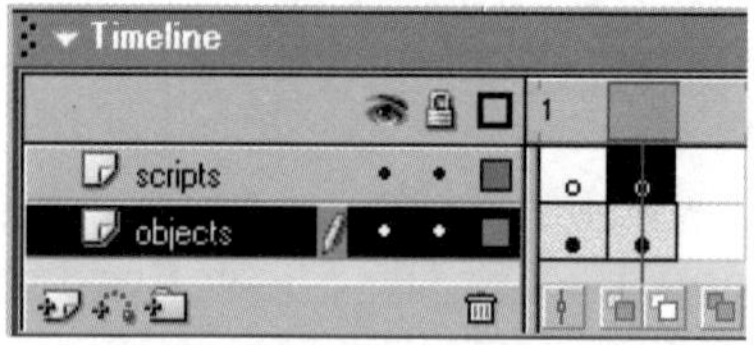

Figure 11.19 Our Timeline so far.

Expert Mode

Select frame 1 in the scripts layer, open the **Actions** panel and click on the **Options** icon and select **Expert Mode**. (We could once again have used **Normal** mode for this next Stage, but let's have a look at how Expert and Normal differ.)

Providing that you have correctly selected frame 1 of the scripts layer, you should see *Actions for Frame 1 of Layer Name scripts* at the top of the Actions panel. Go to **Actions > Movie Control** and double click on **stop**. You will see the command stop(); appear in the script window (Figure 11.20).

Figure 11.20 Double-click on stop to add code to our script window.

If it seems strange to enter a stop command right at the beginning of the movie, remember that if we did not do this, the movie would start playing and move on to frame 2 as soon as it was loaded. The stop command tells the movie to wait on frame 1 until we tell it to do something else.

Now click on your button to select it and from the **Movie Control** menu select **on**. From the resulting menu box select **release** (Figure 11.21).

Take your mouse cursor and click just to the right of the curly bracket on line 1. From the **Movie Control** menu, double click **gotoAndStop**. You will see the command gotoAndStop(); appear in the script window (Figure 11.22). When prompted, enter the number '2' in between the brackets.

Figure 11.21 A pop-up menu appears from which we select release.

Figure 11.22 Our ActionScript is growing.

That takes care of frame 1. We have told Flash to do this: When you load, stay on frame 1 and await orders. If someone clicks on your button, wait until they release it and then go to frame number 2 and stop there.

Now click on Frame 2 in the scripts layer to select it. (At the top of the Actions panel you will see the words *Actions for Frame 2 of Layer Name scripts*.) The joy of working in Expert Mode is that you can type or paste your own blocks of code into the Actions window without having to double click loads of commands. If you know what you are doing, this is very much faster.

Copy the code below into your Actions window, making sure you keep the punctuation exactly as is shown (Figure 11.23):

```
mydate = new Date();
current_time = mydate.getHours();
if (current_time<6) {
greeting = "GOOD EVENING";
}
else if (current_time<12) {
greeting = "GOOD MORNING";
}
else if (current_time<18) {
greeting = "GOOD AFTERNOON";
}
else {
greeting = "GOOD EVENING";
}
hello = greeting;
guest = name;
```

(If we had 'chickened out' we could, if we wanted, create this block of code using the menus in the left hand window of the action panel. It would take a bit of hunting though, but it might be a useful exercise seeing how long it takes you to find the relevant entries.)

What the code does is this: We start by defining a variable named *mydate* and give it the value of **new Date()**. This is an object that constructs a new Date to hold the current date and time, or the date specified.

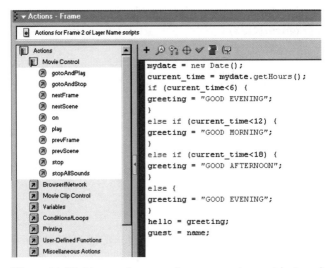

Figure 11.23 Here we have typed our own script straight into the script window.

Next we define a variable named *current_time* and give it the value of **mydate.getHours**. *getHours* is a method that returns the hour as an integer from 0 to 23 of the specified Date object, according to local time. Local time is determined by the operating system on which the Flash Player is running (shown on the bottom right hand corner of your PC's task bar).

`if (current_time<6) { greeting = "GOOD EVENING" }` simply checks the current time and if it is earlier that 06.00 hours (less than 6) an appropriate greeting is created.

else if (current_time<12) { greeting = "GOOD MORNING"; } basi-cally says: or else, if the time is earlier than 12 midday make the greeting say 'Good morning'.

else if (current_time<18) {greeting = "GOOD AFTERNOON";} brings up 'Good Afternoon if the time is earlier than 18.00 hours.

else {greeting = "GOOD EVENING"; } tells Flash that if for some reason it is not possible to determine the PC time, just to say 'Good Evening' regardless!

hello = greeting; takes our dynamic text box named *hello* and applies whatever greeting the script passed across to it. Similarly, guest = name; takes our dynamic text box named *guest* and applies whatever name was entered into the *name* text box in frame 1 to it -i.e. passing the contents of the *name* variable from frame 1 to frame 2.

You can test the movie in the normal way by pressing **Ctrl + Enter** or using the **Test Movie** function from the **Control** menu. A text box will appear asking your visitor to enter a name (Figure 11.24).

Note the use of semi-colons at the end of the ActionScript lines, that are the equivalent of a full stop in normal English.

Enter your name:

Brian

Figure 11.24 When our movie is run we are asked to fill in our name.

Once the name has been entered and the button clicked, a greeting will appear with the name inputted by your visitor appended (Figure 11.25).

GOOD AFTERNOON

Brian

Figure 11.25 Our entered name is now picked up and displayed in frame 2.

In this chapter we have only scratched the surface of the many things that ActionScript is capable of. Unfortunately, we have found that Macromedia's instruction manual and help files are anything but 'user-friendly' and would strongly recommend that you take a look at some of the sample files included with the program to see how they work (go to **Help > Samples**). After that, take a look at some of the Websites recommended at the end of this book which contain loads of examples, downloadable code and tutorials that you can work through.

Flash's ActionScript is not the easiest of things to get to grips with in a hurry, but a little determination pays big dividends when you discover how powerful this scripting language really is.

Publishing your movies

12

Optimising playback

Publishing movies for use on the web

Publishing movies as stand-alone Flash player files

HTML Publishing

Displaying alternative images

Projector files

Other image formats

Printing

OK. We've created our Flash masterpiece and have tested it out using the Test Movie functions incorporated into our editor. The time has now come to publish our Flash movie to allow others to use it.

Flash files can be viewed in a number of different ways, but the basis for everything is the Flash Player Format – or .swf file. This format is the only one that supports all the functions that we have experimented with in creating our Flash project; however, you can export movies into 'lesser' formats such as bitmapped images, animated images, vector files, and so on. They can also be viewed as stand alone 'projector' files. We'll return to all of these shortly.

Up till now we have been able to save our working files as Flash Movie – .fla – files, and it is important to understand the difference between these and the Player format – .swf – files. The former can be thought of as the development file standard. As we develop the movie, everything we create is saved in an all-encompassing Flash Movie file format, which we can return to in order to edit or change settings at any time.

The published Player format file can be set to prohibit editing by anyone else, stopping others from exploring its inner workings. Only the information needed to display the movie is contained in a .swf file.

Optimising playback

Perversely, before we start to export our movies, let's just pause for a moment to consider the all-important question of quality versus quantity. Naturally we want the final movie to be in as high a quality as possible. But, especially if the movie is to be viewed over the Web, there is a price to pay for higher quality, and that is longer download times.

All Web developers know that a happy compromise has to be struck between the quality and size of image files and the time it takes to download that file. That compromise is all the more important in Flash since not only is the download time important so as not to keep your users waiting too long, but if you are using streaming video, the last thing you want is for the movie to stop and start as large chunks of animation try to squeeze down that narrow tube of available bandwidth.

There are many things that affect the overall file size of your final movie. For instance:

- a large number of bitmapped images;
- lots of keyframes;
- sounds;
- embedded fonts;
- gradients instead of plain fills;
- using individual graphic objects instead of symbols or groups.

However, Flash does not leave you to fend for yourself. It can simulate streaming of both video and audio and graphs your bandwidth so you can see at a glance which frames are likely to cause problems. The key to this help can be found when you test your movie (**Control > Test Movie**).

The debug menu of the Flash Player (*not* the editor) has some new options (Figure 12.1), which allow you to set the simulated download speed of a modem. You can see that the three most common modem speeds of 14.4, 28.8 and 56.6 kbps are listed, but you can also set them to whatever download speed you wish to simulate – allowing loading over a company intranet, via ISDN or ADSL, for example.

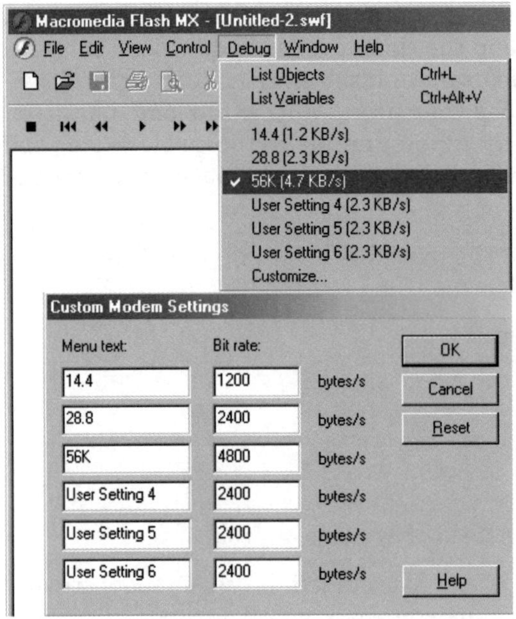

Figure 12.1 Setting your simulated download speed.

Having set the simulated speed, you now need to go to the **View** menu and select **Bandwidth Profiler**. At the top of the screen Flash now presents you with a graph which shows how much information is being transmitted along the Timeline of your movie (Figure 12.2), each bar representing the amount of data in each frame.

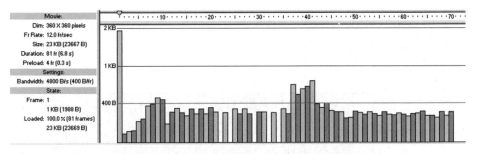

Figure 12.2 At this modem speed setting we may experience some minor pauses.

We've set our modem rate to 56.6 kbps for this example and you will see how a number of frames just nudge over the bottom line (which is coloured red). This warns us that at this particular modem speed these particular frames may cause the movie to pause a fraction while they download. (At a modem speed of 56.6, and with the frame rate set to 12 fps, the available bandwidth equates to around 4800 bytes per second, or 400 bytes per frame. If we had set the frame rate to 30 fps, then the available bandwidth would have been reduced to 4800/30 = 160 bytes per frame; and at this setting the amount of hesitation would be even greater.)

Flash also shows how the movie will stream if we choose **View > Streaming Graph** from the player menu line. Each of the alternate bars of light and dark grey reflect the time taken to download that particular sector of information. When a frame contains very little information, you may well see more than one bar in a single time unit (as in Figure 12.3).

*Flash can generate a printed report of the amount of information contained in your finished movie. When publishing the movie (see below) tick the box marked **Generate size report** under the **Flash** tab of the **Publish Settings** dialog box.*

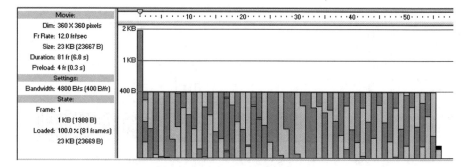

Figure 12.3 In streaming mode the width of the bar indicates how long it takes to download.

If you want to see a graphical representation of your movie actually streaming, go to the **View** menu and select **Show Streaming**. A green bar works its way along the Timeline to show how much has been downloaded in the given time.

Publishing movies for use on the Web

Flash's **Publish** command is used to create all the files necessary to view your Flash project file, even if the end user does not have a Flash player to view the finished file. As well as preparing a Flash Player (.swf) file, Publish can also create alternative image formats (such as GIF, JPEG, PNG and QuickTime) for use on the web in the event that the Flash Player is not available and the user cannot (or will not) download the necessary player from the Web. All the HTML code necessary to embed the finished file within a Web document is created automatically and Publish can also generate stand-alone projectors for both the Windows and Macintosh computer systems.

When deciding on the formats that you wish Flash to generate you need to access the **Publish Settings** dialog box from the **File** menu (Figure 12.4). This allows you to publish in up to eight different formats as well as create the necessary HTML code for displaying the finished files in a browser.

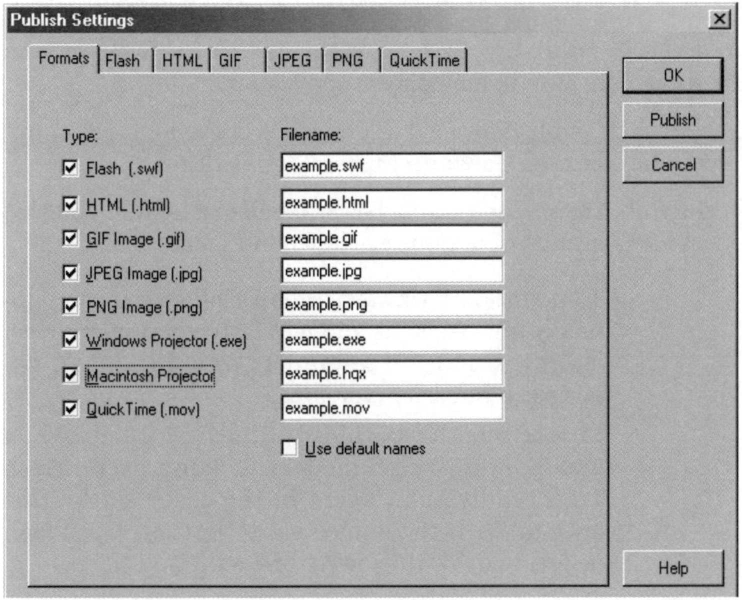

Figure 12.4 Selecting the Publish settings.

Having chosen your preferred formats, you can instruct Flash to publish your movie by clicking on the **Publish** button on the top right corner of the dialog box, or by going to the **File** menu at a later time and selecting **Publish**. The published files are all stored in the same directory location as the original movie.

Publishing your movies as stand-alone Flash player files

As well as allowing you to publish your movies for use on the Web, or in a browser, Flash can also create stand-alone player applications.

First you need to select your publish options as described above and make sure that the **Flash (.swf)** checkbox (as shown in Figure 12.4) is ticked.

The second tab in the Publish Settings dialog box is labelled **Flash**. Open this dialog box and you should see a list of options as shown in Figure 12.5.

Version	To maintain backwards compatibility you can publish your work as older Flash version movies. However, many of the functions of Flash MX will not work in earlier versions.
Load Order	This affects the download of the first frame. When a slow network or modem is being used, Flash draws individual layers in the order set by this option. With the choice set to Bottom Up, Flash begins to draw the lowest levels first.
Generate size report	This option generates a printed report about the size of your movie.

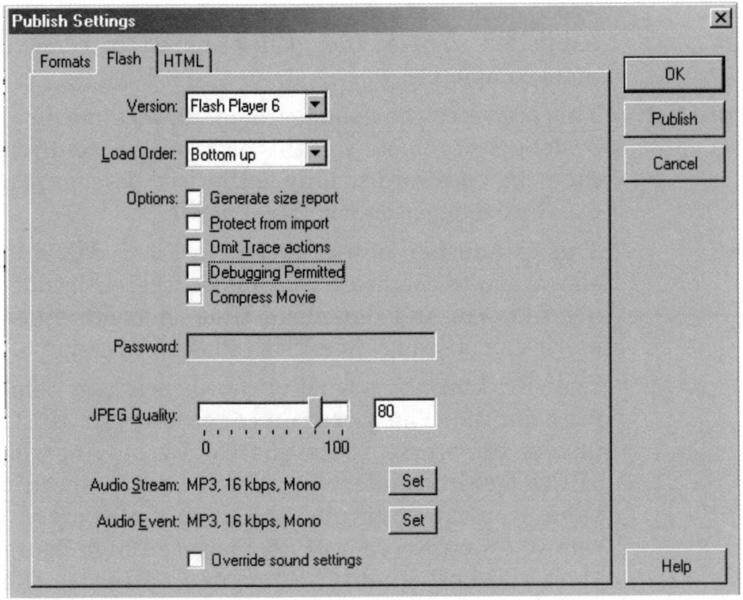

Figure 12.5 Setting options for your Flash Player file.

Protect from import   By ticking here you can prevent others from importing your movie back into a Flash editor without first entering a **Password** (set in the box beneath the checkboxes).

Omit trace actions   Trace comments add to the final size of your published movie file. Click here to remove them completely.

Debugging Permitted   This activates the debugger and allows a movie to be debugged remotely. If this option is selected you can set a password so only authorised persons can use the debugger on your final movie.

Compress Movie   This is another new addition to Flash MX and allows you to compress your movie, thereby reducing file size and download time. A compressed movie can only play in a Flash Player of version 6.

JPEG Quality   The JPEG format is what is known as a lossy compression file. The more you compress your JPEG image, the worse is its quality. By moving the JPEG Quality slider (or by entering a specific value) you can determine the amount of compression you want for your JPEG images. A high figure gives the best quality; a low one optimises the download time.

Audio Stream Event   Use these buttons to override the rate and compression levels both for streaming and event sounds (see Figure 12.6). Obviously for these settings to work there have to be sounds present in your movie! The compression pop-up menu gives you five choices: **ADPCM** is used for short event sounds. **MP3** is used when you have mainly longer streaming sounds. At settings lower than 20 kbps all sounds are played in mono, regardless of whether there was stereo content to begin with. A **Raw** setting causes no sound compression to be applied. **Speech** limits the sampling rate to a maximum of 44 kHz. And **Disable** switches off sound altogether.

Override sound settings The above settings will defer to your original choice of sound compression unless this check box is ticked. This could be useful if you wanted to create two versions of your movie: one lower quality one for Web use and another higher quality stand-alone version.

Figure 12.6 The Sound Settings dialog box.

HTML publishing

In order to play a Flash movie in a Web browser it is necessary to create the code to embed the .swf file into an HTML document.

By filling in blanks in a template depending on your choice of options, Flash can do a whole load of clever things such as detecting whether the browser used is capable of playing Flash movies and automatically downloading a player from the Web if necessary.

The HTML options are set using the **Publish Settings** choice in the **File** menu and selecting the tab marked **HTML** (see Figure 12.7).

Template

You can choose from the drop-down menu one of a number of templates to use in creating your HTML file. The simplest template to use is the one called **Flash Only**. This only allows users who have browsers equipped with the Flash Player to see your movie. Other viewers will be unable to see it. Some of the other template choices, however, create HTML code that displays alternative images if the Flash Player is not present. To find out what each template offers, click on the **Info** button to the right of the menu after you have made a selection.

Dimensions

This option is used to determine the size of your final movie when played in the browser. The default is **Match Movie**, which sets the dimensions to those of the movie itself; but you can also choose to size the movie as an exact number of pixels wide and high, or as a percentage of the browser window.

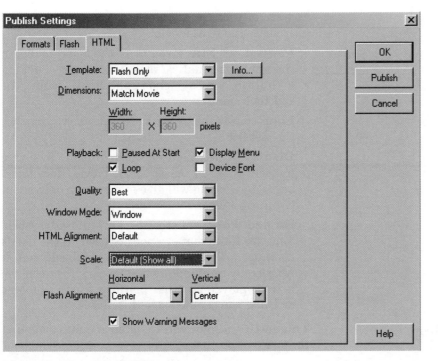

Figure 12.7 Setting the HTML options.

Playback

You are offered four choices to determine how the user views the final movie:

Paused at Start requires the user to begin the movie manually – most probably by clicking a button or by choosing **Play** from the shortcut menu.

Loop causes the movie to repeat when it reaches the last frame.

Display Menu makes a shortcut menu available to users who right click on the movie. If switched off, right clicking will give information only about the Flash Player.

Device Font substitutes anti-aliased system fonts for fonts that are not installed on the user's computer. This can speed up playback, but it works only on Windows systems; so if your movie is to be played on other platforms such as a Mac or Unix, you should leave this unselected.

Quality

This setting allows you to balance quality against the speed of playback.

Low switches anti-aliasing off permanently

Autolow allows Flash to switch on anti-aliasing if it finds that your computer can handle the downloading of individual frames.

Autohigh assumes that anti-aliasing should be turned on unless the user's computer is unable to keep up with frame downloads.

High gives priority to appearance over playback speed. With no animation, bitmaps are smoothed; otherwise they are not.

Best smoothes all bitmaps and anti-aliasing is always switched on.

Window Mode

For Windows users you can allow your movie's transparency options to permit other elements to move behind the movie using Dynamic HTML and either be hidden by the movie (**Opaque** setting) or show through (**Transparent Windowless**). This option is not available for users of other operating systems and Windows users must be using Internet Explorer v4 or above with the Flash Active X control.

HTML Alignment

You can specify whether you want your movie aligned within the browser window on the Left, Right, Top or Bottom.

Scale

If you specify width and height settings which are different from the movie's original size, you can determine whether Flash resizes the movie keeping the aspect ratio of the original, or whether it stretches either or both sides of the movie to be an exact fit within the browser frame.

Flash Alignment	These settings determine how the movie is placed within its own window.
Show Warning Messages	Flash can display a warning if there are any conflicts in the tag settings.

Displaying alternative images

Quite often on the Web there will be people browsing who don't want to go to the bother of downloading a plug-in if their browser does not already support that standard, or who have switched off Flash movies within their browser to speed up download times. In such cases, Flash can substitute animated or still images so that your viewer is not forced to look at a blank screen, or part of screen.

GIF images

If you have simple Web animations, you could, for instance, substitute animated GIF files, which might take longer to download than the original Flash file, but would at least offer something to see. In your Publish Settings dialog box, select the checkbox marked **GIF** (see Figure 12.4). A new tab appears at the top of the box marked **GIF**, which you should now open (Figure 12.8).

Once again, there are a number of options you can choose for your GIF file (Figure 12.8).

Choosing the GIF option will also automatically generate the necessary code in the resulting HTML file for substituting a GIF image if the Flash file cannot be played. The same is true of JPEG and PNG files.

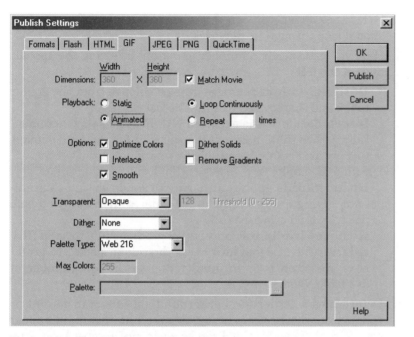

Figure 12.8 The GIF settings in the Publish Settings dialog box.

Dimensions   You can choose to have the GIF file the same size as the movie, or to determine the width and height of the image.

Playback   You can choose whether you want a single static image to be substituted, or the entire animation exported as an animated

	GIF. If the latter, you can then determine how many times it should loop through its playback.
Options	Here you can specify a number of options affecting the appearance of the GIF:

> **Optimize colors** removes unused colours from the colour table, and thereby reduces the file size.
>
> **Interlace** allows the exported GIF file to display incrementally rather than making the user wait for the entire image to download before being able to view it.
>
> **Smooth** enables or disables anti-aliasing.
>
> **Dither Solids** applies dithering to solids as well as gradients, giving a seemingly larger palette than the Web-safe palette would otherwise allow.
>
> **Remove Gradients** converts all gradient fills to solid fills, reducing file size and improving the colour since GIF gradients are often poor in quality due to the low number of available colours.

Transparent	Determines whether the background appears transparent or opaque, or whether colours below an alpha threshold appear transparent. This threshold can be given any number between 0 and 255. It is often a good idea to experiment with this setting.
Dither	Here you can specify which type of dithering, if any, you wish Flash to perform in order to approximate to all the colours with only a limited colour palette. **Ordered** provides the best dithering for the least possible file size increase. **Diffusion** creates the best dithering irrespective of file size.

Palette Type You can specify whether to use the **Web 216**-safe standard colour palette or customise the palette to your own specifications. The latter option often results in larger file sizes.

Max Colors If you select **Adaptive** or **Web Snap** options as your palette type, you can determine the maximum number of colours to be used in your GIF file.

JPEG and PNG images, and QuickTime movies

Just as the GIF tab gives you a selection of options to choose from, so too do the JPEG and PNG tabs in the Publish Settings dialog box. The options are very similar, and therefore it should not be necessary for us to go through each of the settings again.

Suffice it to say, however, that whereas GIF files are ideal for line art drawings where there are large amounts of block colour, JPEGs are better for photographs and images that include gradients. In addition, the former are normally limited to 216 colours whereas JPEG files use the whole 16 million-colour palette.

PNG files can also support transparency (alpha channels), and although their use is still limited on the World Wide Web, most of the later browsers can happily cope with them.

QuickTime movies can be recognised both by Windows and Macintosh systems. Flash MX creates QuickTime 4 format movies and these can recognise Flash's interactive features.

Projector files

For those who will view your movies without using a browser, Flash can create self-contained movie files, which play without the aid of external programs. Projector files are self-sufficient in that they contain everything needed to replay a Flash movie.

To create a projector file for Windows or Mac simply tick the checkbox(es) in the Publish Settings dialog box. There are no options to select for projector files, but Flash creates an .exe file for Windows users or an .hqx file for Mac users (Figure 12.9).

example.fla   example.swf   example.exe   example.hqx

Figure 12.9 Windows and Mac projector files together with the original 'fla' file and the Shockwave (swf) file.

Other image formats

As well as exporting Flash movies as SWF, JPEG, GIF and PNG images, you can also export individual frames as:

- EPS (Encapsulated PostScript);
- AI (Illustrator);
- PICT (Mac PICT);

- BMP (Windows Bitmap);
- WMF (Windows Metafile);
- EMF (Enhanced Metafile);
- DXF (Autocad DXF);
- SPL (FutureSplash Player);
- SWT (Generator Template).

You can achieve any of these exports by going to the **File** menu and selecting **Export Image**. Alternatively, to export the movie as a sequence of frames, go to **File > Export Movie**. In addition to the above formats you can export to:

- AVI (Windows Audio Visual);
- WAV (WAV audio);
- MOV (QuickTime Movie).

Printing

When developing your movie, Flash allows you to print out individual frames – or a number of frames together, somewhat as a storyboard layout – from the .fla file

From the **File** menu of the editor, choose **Page Setup** to determine page size, margins and whether you want the printer to print in portrait or landscape mode (Figure 12.10).

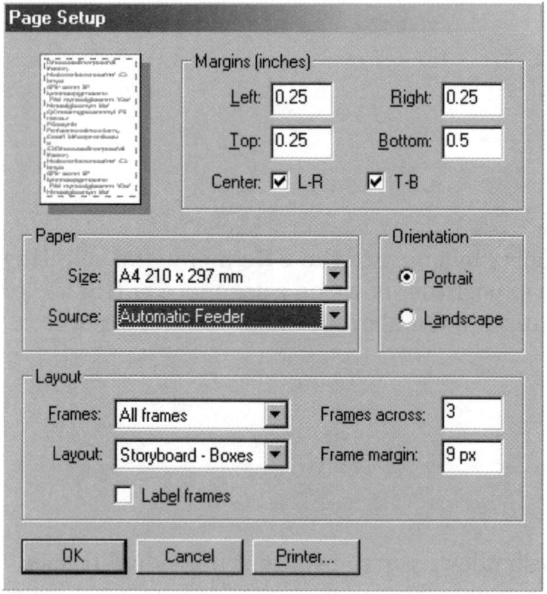

Figure 12.10 The Page Setup menu.

In the layout boxes you can choose whether you want to print out just the first frame or a selection of frames. If the latter, you should select **All frames** and then choose which pages you wish to print in the **Print** dialog box (Figure 12.11). The last drop-down menu in Figure 12.10 (**Layout**) allows you to specify whether you print out individual frames as single pages or as storyboard layouts.

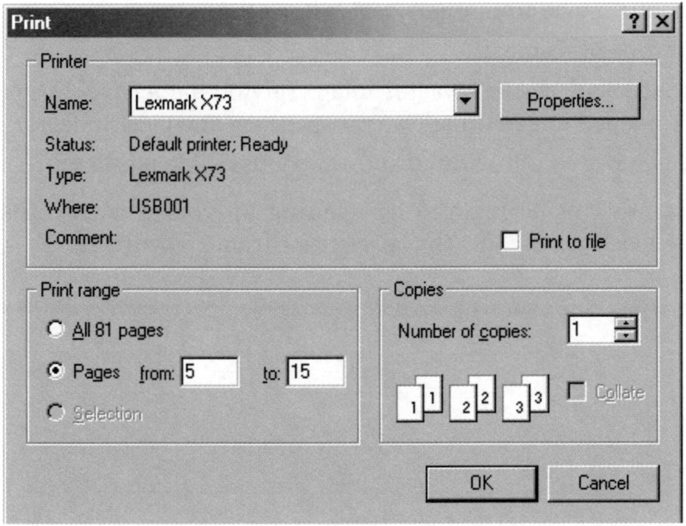

Figure 12.11 Determine which pages you want to print out from the Print dialog box.

*You can choose to print each frame number underneath their individual thumbnail images by selecting the **Label frames** check box in Page Setup when you choose one of the Storyboard options.*

Printing from a Flash movie

With the previous version of Flash came the introduction of one particular standard facility that many thought was long overdue in earlier versions: that of being able to print particular pages from the movie that could be specified by the movie's author. But in addition, the new facility allowed you to:

*To publish a movie with specific frames labelled for printing, the movie must be viewed with Flash Player version 4.0.25 or later. You can use a JavaScript routine to check for your users' player version, which Macromedia provides as part of its Deployment Kit. You can download this directly from the web at **http://www.macrome-dia.com/software/flash/download/**.*

- protect material in your movie from unauthorised printing;
- determine the print area of frames;
- specify if the printout should be as a vector image (giving higher resolution printing) or as a bitmapped image (to allow transparency and other effects);
- allow something to be printed out without it even being visible on screen!

You specify which frames can be printed by opening up your **Properties Panel** and entering '*#p*' as the label for that particular frame (Figure 12.12).

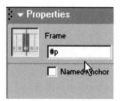

Figure 12.12 You specify printable frames in the Frame Panel.

It may well be that you don't want the entire movie area to print out, but just a small section of the screen. No problem! Create a frame that will not be viewed as part of the movie (perhaps at the very end of the Timeline) and create a shape, the size of the area you want printed. This time you should enter '*#b*' in the Properties Frame Label panel. You can only do this once per Timeline, and your bounding box will affect all printable frames in that Timeline.

If you specifically don't want *any* frames to be printed out by your end users, insert '*!#p*' in any frame's panel box. This also has the effect of dimming the *print* command from the right-click context menu.

You can, if you like, assign the '#p' label to a frame as part of a button instruction so that the movie frames print when you click on the button.

Conclusion

Now that you have reached the end of this book you are only at the beginning of discovering the many and varied things you can do with Flash MX. Some of the tasks may look daunting at first, but experimentation really does make for familiarity, and we cannot over-emphasise how versatile and essential this package is for anyone wishing to create first rate dynamic Websites and interactive movies.

For inspiration, you might like to visit the following Websites that use Flash extensively. Some provide sample code that you can try out, which is always a good way to learn new software by 'unpicking' other people's offerings:

- **www.macromedia.com/software/flash** – Macromedia's own resource site and a good starting off point.
- **www.thelinkz.com** – Site devoted to Flash MX resources.
- **http://actionscript-toolbox.com** – Resource site devoted to ActionScript.
- **http://board.flashkit.com/board** – discussion forum on MX.
- **http://graphicssoft.about.com/cs/flash** – tutorials, downloads and resources for beginners, intermediate and advanced users.
- **www.actionscripts.org** – An on-line Flash MX community.
- **www.flashpro.nl** – a Dutch site with masses of downloads.
- **www.webthang.co.uk** – Tutorials and downloads.

Good luck in your creativity. The (animated) ball is now in your court!

Index

A

abstract variables, 199
action frames, assignment of, 151
actions, 150
    previewing of, 158–9
    see also frame actions
ActionScript, 10, 188–212
Adobe Illustrator, 71
AI format, 232
alignment of objects, 56–7
Alpha settings, 112, 131
alternative images for display on
    the Web, 228
anchors, 155
animated masks, 144–5
animations, 116
    frame-by-frame, 121–7
    saving of, 145–7
    see also motion tweening; shape
        tweening
anti-aliasing, 63, 226–7, 230
Arrow tool, 42–4, 50

Autolow and Autohigh settings,
    226–7
AVI format, 233

B

Bandwidth Profiler, 216–17
BarChart component, 200
bitmapped images, 6–7, 69, 72
    converted to vector elements, 73–4
    painting with, 75–9
BMP format, 233
Break Apart option, 65–6
Brush tool and Brush mode, 35–7
buttons, 159–69
    creation of, 160–4
    events triggered by, 168–9
    for interactity, 164–9
    sound added to, 176–7

C

Calendar component, 201
CGI commands, 191
checkerboard pattern, 44

circles, drawing of, 20
Clipboard, importing from, 71–2
Color Threshold for vector images,
    74–5
colour gradients, 22, 32–3, 231
    removal of, 230
colour selection, 21–3
    for GIF files, 231
    for instances, 112–13
    for outlines on layers, 89–90
    using motion tweening, 131–2
colour swatches, 33
comments about frames, 154–5
components, 197, 200–1
compression, 172, 222
concrete variables, 199
Copy command, 48–9
corner points, creation of, 51
Corner Threshold for vector
    images, 74
cross-hair pointer, 29
Ctrl+A, 44

Ctr+Alt+C, 120
Ctr+Alt+V, 120
Ctrl+Shift+O, 102
Ctrl+Shift+V, 100
Curve Fit for vector images, 74
Cut command, 48–9

D
debugging, 215, 222
Deployment Kit, 236
deselection of objects, 47
device fonts, 63
dimensions of movies, 14, 224
distribution of objects, 57
dithering, 230
download time, 214–17
Drag Over and Drag Out events, 168
DraggablePane component, 201
Dropper tool, 76–7
duplication of objects, 49
DXF format, 233

E
Easing value, 133, 138
Edit Multiple Frames option, 125–6
editing commands, 48–9
Editor, 8–9
ellipses, drawing of, 20
e-mail from within a movie, 193–7
embedded fonts, 63

EMF format, 233
EPS format, 232
Eraser tool, 37–9
evenly-spaced objects, 57
event sounds, 172, 180, 222
.exe files, 232
Expert Mode, 194–5, 206–12
expressions, 199
Extension Manager, 200–1

F
fading in and out
    of objects, 131
    of sound, 183
Faucet tool, 37–8
file formats acceptable to Flash MX,
    68–9
fills, 18
Fireworks software, 71
.fla files, 214
Flash Only template, 224
Flash Player, 4, 214
flipping
    of objects, 54–5
    of text blocks, 65
focus, setting and killing of, 168
folders, 12, 84, 91, 105–6, 174–5
font selection, 61–3
frame actions, 150–3

frame numbers, 12, 235
frame rate, 13, 126–7, 180
frames 116–17
    comments on, 154–5
    insertion of, 120
    labelling of, 153–5, 235–7
    previewing of, 128
    removal of, 121
    reversal of, 143–4
    sound added to, 175–6
    stepping through, 122
    see also keyframes
Free Transform tool, 52–3
freehand drawing, 27

G
gaps, closing of, 34
getURL command, 193–4, 199–202
GIF files, 7, 218, 228–31
Go To action, 157
gradients see colour gradients
graphics
    animated, 146
    imported into Flash MX, 68
grids, 15
grouping of objects, 57–8
guide layers and guided layers, 91,
    95–6
guidelines, 96

H

'hit' states, 163–4
hot spots, 164, 176
.hqx files, 232
HTML documents, 224–8
hyperlinks, creation of, 189–92

I

IconButton component, 201
import
    of graphics into Flash MX, 68
    protection of movies from, 221
    of raster graphics, 69–71
    of sounds, 173–5
    of vector-based graphics, 71
    via the clipboard, 71–2
Info panel, 48, 53
Ink Bottle tool, 39–40
Ink mode, 27
installation of Flash MX, 2–6
instances, 102, 107–14 *passim*
    making changes to, 110–14
interactivity
    formulaic, 188
    using buttons, 164–9
interlacing, 230
invisible buttons, 169
invisible layers, 88

J

JPEG files, 222, 228, 231

K

kerning, 62
keyframes, 117–21

L

labels for frames, 153–5, 235–7
Lasso tool, 44–6
layers, 12, 84–100
    controlled by Timeline, 92–3
    creation and deletion of, 87–8
    height of, 89, 174
    naming of, 85–6
    setting parameters for, 88–92
    stacking of objects in, 93–5
libraries, 102–7, 173, 175
line spacing, 62
Line tool, 18–20
LineChart component, 200
locking of layers, 88
looping movies, 226
looping sound, 180
lossy compression, 222

M

Magic Wand tool, 80–1
margins, 62
mask layers and masked layers, 91,
    96–9
masks, animated 144–5
Match, 14

Match Movie, 224
Match Size, 57
MessageBox component, 201
Minimum Area for vector images,
    74–5
morphing, 128, 136–43 *passim*
motion guides and motion paths,
    134–6
motion tweening, 127–34
    for changing colour, 132
    for changing size, 132–3
    combined with shape tweening, 143
    for moving objects, 127–30
    for rotating objects, 133–4
MOV format, 233
movie clips, 146–7, 160
MP3 format, 172, 222–3

N

named anchors, 155
null colour, 21–2

O

objects, creation of, 18
Onion Skin facility, 122–5
opaque instances, 112
optimisation of movie playback,
    214–18
'Orient to path' option, 135
Oval tool, 20–1

P

padlock icon, 93, 99
Paint Bucket tool, 31–4
painting with bitmapped images, 75–9
panels, 10
passing variables, 203–6
Paste command, 48–9
Paste in Place, 49, 100
Paste Special, 50, 72
Pen tool, 28–30
Pencil tool, 25–8
photographic images, 73–4, 231
PICT files, 232
PieChart component, 200
Play action, 156
playback of movies
    optimisation of, 214–18
    options for, 226, 229
PNG files, 228, 231
Polygon mode, 45–6
portions of elements, selection of, 46
positioning of objects, 47–8
Press button event, 168
previewing
    of actions, 158–9
    of frames, 128
printing
    from Flash movies, 235–6
    of frames, 233–4
    prevention of, 237

Stage area matched for, 14
ProgressBar component, 201
projector files, 232
Property Inspector, 10
publication of movies, 218–20, 236
    as HTML documents, 224–8
    as stand-alone Flash Player files,
    220–3

Q

QuickTime movies, 69, 172, 231

R

raster graphics, 7, 69–71
Rectangle tool, 22–5
reference points, 96
registration points, 48
Release and Release Outside events,
    168
reorientation of objects, 54–5
repositioning of objects, 47–8
reshaping of filled areas, 51–2
resizing of objects, 52–4
    by motion tweening, 132–3
reversal of frames, 143–4
Roll Over and Roll Out events, 168
Rotate and Skew icon, 54–5
rotation
    of objects, 133–4
    of text, 63–5
rulers and ruler units, 12–15

S

_sans font, 63
Scale and Rotate command, 52–3
scenes, 147–8
scrollbars, 198
segments
    making changes to, 50–1
    selection of, 42–4
selection of objects, 42–6
sequential files, import of, 70–1
serial number of software, 3
_serif font, 63
shape creation, 18
shape hints, 141–2
shape tweening, 136–9
    combined with motion tweening,
    143
    with multiple objects, 140–1
Shockwave format (.swf) files, 156,
    191, 214
size reports, 218, 220
skewing
    of objects, 54–5
    of text blocks, 65
smoothing
    of animations, 122–5
    of curves, 27
snap features, 15, 96
solid points, 28

sound, 172–85
   added to buttons, 176–7
   added to frames, 175–6
   editing of files, 182–5
   import of, 173–5
sound events, 177–9
SPL format, 233
SplitView component, 201
stacking
   of actions, 169
   of objects, 93–5
Stage area, 10, 13
start sounds, 179–80
Stop action, 156
storyboard layouts, 234–5
Straighten mode, 27
streaming sounds, 172, 180–1
streaming video, 8, 215, 218
strokes, 18
Subselection tool, 30
Swap Symbol dialog box, 113–14
SWT format, 233
symbols, 102–6
   created directly, 108–9
   created from graphic objects, 107–8
   used in preference to objects,
      109–10

Sync settings, 177–8
system requirements for Flash MX, 2

T

testing of movies, 15–16
text
   displayed vertically, 63–4
   insertion of, 60–1
text blocks, width of, 61
thumbnail images, 235
Ticker component, 201
.tif files, 7
Timeline, 10–12
   hiding of, 12
   size of, 119–20
   used to control layers, 92–3
Toolbar, 10, 14
tooltips, 14–15
Topspin Group, xv
Transform Fill, 33–4, 78–9
Transform panel, 54–5
transparency
   of instances, 112
   in movies, 230
   of objects, 131
Tree component, 201
triggering of action, 168
tweening 129; *see also* motion
      tweening; shape tweening

type
   attributes, 61–4
   converted into objects, 65–6
   transformation of, 65
_typewriter font, 63

U

uniform resource locators (URLs), 190
Use Counts, 106

V

variables, 196, 199, 203–6
vector graphics, 6–8
   derived from bitmaps, 73–4
   import of, 71
vertically-displayed text, 63–4
volume of sound, 183

W

WAV files, 172, 233
Web pages, loading of, 191
'Web safe' colours, 21–2, 231
Websites making use of Flash, 238
window states, 192
WMF format, 233
word wrap, 60
work area in Editor, 10